****

I met Maureen in 2001 in Egypt. Having been born and-off for 30 years, and having written seven documentaries on ancient Egypt and its monume Egypt well. Thus I can also say with conviction incarnate model of a true priestess of ancient .
smart, witty, deeply perceptive, a beautiful lady inside and out, has a huge open-heart, and most of all she has acquired a vast wisdom of life and human relationships, as well as a great knowledge of sacred geometry, that is very inspirational to all those who have had the good fortune to read her new book, Be A Genie. We can direct our destiny and dreams, and Maureen has understood how to do it.

Robert G. Bauval
Best-Selling Author of *The Orion Mystery* & *Message of the Sphinx*

****

*I love your book, **Be a Genie**. For the first time I understand what sacred geometry is and how to use it. I have read dozens of books about Sacred Geometry. You have grounded your ideas with math and science in a way that is clear and practical. The summaries at the end of each chapter were invaluable to me. I do not have a mathematical background. Using your summaries I was able to carry the essential ideas from chapter to chapter and build on them.*

I treasure this book and it has become a central tool for me in my life. I have shared concepts and ideas contained in it with others and they can't wait to buy the book. Thank God for your brilliance but thank you for making these metaphysical ideas so practical and user friendly.

Ingrid Dilley
Author, Facilitator, Trainer
Renewing Life Program
Madison, WI

****

I'm normally pretty unenthusiastic about self-development books, but Maureen has produced one with some real rigor to it... She has backed up her book in a unique way, with sacred geometry and related matters, which distinguishes it from the general standard.

John Anthony West
Best-Selling Author of books on Egypt including,
Serpent in the Sky: The High Wisdom of Ancient Egypt

****

****

Maureen St. Germain has brought a fresh perspective to the ancient spiritual science of sacred geometry. Clearly the many remarkable insights in **Be a Genie** *are those of someone who has a deep personal commitment to the wisdom principles which inspired the nearly forgotten science of a lost fountainhead of civilization.*

From many sources, including her own rich experience, she has assembled a guidebook to some of sacred geometry's greatest secrets and their application to modern personal challenges. The book should prove a valuable resource to anyone-from beginners to the more advanced-interested in probing beyond today's standard superficialities.

Particularly interesting are her observations on what she calls the Phoenix sequence. In a time of psycho-babble and political correctness it is indeed refreshing to read something rooted in the timeless principles which remain as relevant to the human soul today as they have since the dawn of awareness on this planet. Good fortune.

Doug Kenyon
Editor
Atlantis Rising Magazine

****

Ms. St. Germain in her new book, **Be a Genie,** *has been able to give us a basic introduction to the chaos theory, multiple possibilities and to quantum physics. The new age adage of "we create our own reality "has been given a more scientific rationale by her explanations. It gives us the nuts and bolts of how to create our reality; it is a blueprint for the development of our future. For those who have taken basic courses in Sacred Geometry, "Genie" brings back the concepts in a simple easily understood manner.*

It should be required reading for your courses on the Genie and advisable for all your students of Sacred Geometry.

Joe Mather, MD
Retired

****

BE A GENIE

Create Love, Success and Happiness

Maureen J. St. Germain

Phoenix Rising Publishing

New York, NY

BE A GENIE

Create Love, Success and Happiness

by

Maureen J. St. Germain

Published by

Phoenix Rising Publishing

559 W. 183rd St., B-1

New York, NY 10033

Phoenix Rising Publishing is a division of Transformational Enterprises, Inc.

www.MaureenStGermain.com

Editor: Larry Skrenes

ISBN 978-0-9911898-3-0

Printed in the United States of America

****

Most of my adult life has been devoted to the numbers of sacred geometry and their application to the stock markets and currency markets of the world-it was not until I met Maureen St Germain that the true nature of these amazing number sequences became even more useful to me.

Maureen presents these numbers in an easy to understand format-it is a step by step journey to enlightenment using these numbers-the book is simple to understand and will open the eyes to both the novice and expert-the incredible harmony in all the universe will be readily apparent before you finish the book.

As I studied these numbers in my search to consistently beat the stock market, I was led to the works of Sir Isaac Newton. Sir Isaac was so enthralled about the power behind the Fibonacci sequence he had the spiral mirabilis diagram carved in the oak headboard of his bed.

Newton seemed to believe that the answer to reincarnation was in that spiral. Put a genie at work for you-it will enhance your life.

Larry Pesavento
Author of 21 books on Sacred Geometry & the Stock Market
TradingTutor.com

****

You deserve high praise for your work. It's brilliant! I've only read the first part so far and have been very impressed with your ability to take complex concepts and make them understandable. I'm so excited to connect with someone who, like myself, is trying to correlate science and spirituality. I look forward to visiting with you after I finish the book and share some of the information that's come in to me that dove tails with your work.

I love your analogies. Thanks again for your wonderful book! I'm looking forward to finishing it. It's exciting to find someone of like mind I can actually converse with about this without their eyes rolling back in their head and the shades going down.

Claudia Nelson
Retired Schoolteacher & Author

****

****

In August of 2002, I finished my Masters of Education degree and was scheduled to graduate when a friend invited me to attend Maureen's "Genie in the Bottle" Workshop. Even though I had practiced manifesting since early childhood, I decided to attend the Class rather than attend my own graduation ceremony. My goal and hope was to learn new techniques, ask questions, and perfect my skills as I continued manifesting different aspects of my life. I was hoping that Maureen could tell me where I was 'going wrong' and how I 'could improve' in one or two areas. Also, I wanted to gain a better understanding of how the process of manifesting actually works.

The Class exceeded my expectations and I have been pleased with the knowledge and techniques gained. Thanks to Maureen, I not only have an understanding of how the process works; I also have perfected my skills. I immediately began manifesting a job with my perfect place of employment in mind. Within 2 weeks, I received offers from three employers, one of which happened to be the perfect job that I had manifested. It was the office where I had worked as an Intern for 1 year during graduate school but had previously been told there was no openings. Needless to say, I was overjoyed to be working at the Counseling Center where I received training! That was just the beginning of improvements as I learned to practice just one new skill I learned from Maureen-keeping negatives out of manifesting.

In short, did the Class with Maureen change my life? I will let you decide ... over the past year ... I have packed and moved from my home of 10 years to a location 200 miles away, changed jobs, started a career as motivational speaker, married the man of my dreams, traveled through Europe for a month-long honeymoon, worked through 3 family issues that have plagued me for 30 years, restored my grandparent's old house, and found the courage to place my teenage son in treatment for his behavior.

I would recommend Maureen's class to anyone who is tired of life just happening 'to them'-to anyone interested in creating the life of their dreams. If you are tired of just dreaming and ready to start living out those dreams, this may be what you are looking for. Maureen is an empathic woman with down-to-earth-warmth and a caring attitude toward her students. She is multi-talented and enjoys conveying her knowledge and wisdom to her students. Maureen is passionate about her work and teachings and it shows in her every word and movement.

Debi Williams, M.Ed.
Counseling & Ed. Psychology
Carrollton Georgia
Participant in August 2002 Class in Atlanta

****

This book is dedicated to Mohamed Nazmy

who lit a fire inside of me to finish it.

Using the *Genie System*, life will appear to be magical because you will be in the rhythm and flow of the game of life. You will no longer be an outsider wishing to join in and accidentally end up being pulled in by surprise. The Universe expects you to join in the game by giving you synchronicity to tell you that you are **in** the game, and the *Genie System* teaches you to understand and apply the rules!

Credits

First, I would like to thank my first book agent, Bill Gladstone, who signed me, sight unseen, by reading the manuscript someone handed to him. Bill, you are a Genie in your own right and deserve huge accolades! I am so grateful for the magic you weave in your world, and that I get to be a part of it! It was an honor and pleasure to work with you. I wish to thank the many workshop participants who supported this work with their emails and calls. There are many individuals that I would like to thank whose names didn't make it into these pages. All of them know the part they played. If you think you were one of those people, you probably were!

Special thanks go to Christine McDonough, G. L. Williams, Larry Pesavento, Tim Broder, John O'Neal, Donus Stroufe, Brian and Joanne Jones, Sandi LeGullion, Richard Gerhart, Bev Hays, Robert Bauval, Jon-Paul Bauval, Philippe de Fouchier and family and Debbie Ashworth Williams for her incredible story and life that she lived to her fullest.

Next, I wish to acknowledge my very talented editor of the first edition, Billii Roberti. You helped me get to first base. I remember getting an email from her one time while we were working on yet another edit. I was at home when I lived in Wisconsin and she wrote, "Maureen, I can hear you screaming all the way here in New York."

Extra special thanks go to my editor and friend, Larry Skrenes. Your presence in my life is a God-send. The way you demanded clarity, consistently supported me, and always "showed up" has made this two-year edit a magical journey.

Finally, I wish to thank my darling husband, a physicist, whose technical editing added the feedback I've always wanted from a scientist. You are the BEST.

Thank you, God, for sending all the perfect people to work with me.

Maureen J. St. Germain

www.MaureenStGermain.com

maureen@maureenstgermain.com

Author of best-selling *Beyond the Flower of Life* and *Reweaving the Fabric of Your Reality,* Maureen's book, *Be a Genie,* has been re-released with this update for audiences worldwide. Leading workshops and guiding tours since 1994, Maureen St. Germain's focus is in personal development and spiritual awakening. She is insightful, compassionate, intuitive and funny.

Maureen's vocation is to share the knowledge she has gained from many years studying ancient wisdom. *Be a Genie* is her distillation of this information into a formula for creating your destiny. Her first presentation of this workshop was in 1995 to a standing-room-only audience at a national association meeting. This encouraged her to begin a new career as a workshop facilitator.

Since that time, Maureen has expanded her workshop offerings to include *MerKaBa Classic, Reweaving the Fabric of Your Reality, Be a Genie,* and Akashic Records workshops. These high-caliber seminars assist the participant on his or her path of self-discovery.

She is also the author, writer, voice and musical composer of the over 15 best-selling meditation CDs, such as *MerKaBa II* and the two-CD set, *Sounds from the Great Pyramid,* recorded live in the Great Pyramid of Giza, Egypt. Maureen continues to create new CDs as her work expands. She is also the author of the best-selling MerKaBa Classic DVD set.

Maureen is the mother of four adult sons and is a former nonprofit CEO, fundraiser and lobbyist. She has made several successful career changes in her life. She had been a talk show host on local TV, and now leads workshops throughout the world, as well as Akashic Records International and a number of other organizations.

Maureen considers herself a facilitator, rather than a teacher, in helping you to remember what you already know.

My mission is to assist you in becoming the Highest you can be in any given moment. I intend to be an inspiration to all with whom I come in contact, and to give you, my co-workers on this planet, a lifetime sense of self, along with a passion and compassion for all of life. **- Maureen**

BE A GENIE

Table of Contents

Chapters

Prologue – My Story

Today is my birthday. I'm turning 50 and I have to work. But who is complaining? Everyone in my group had to get up at six so that we could leave for the docks at 7 AM and load into the boat by 8. We'll be in the water with the dolphins by 9 or 10 AM.

The dolphins are wild and swim where they want, but today is a MOST magical day! Lots of dolphins have come to play with us. On some dolphin excursions they don't show up at all, or we have very small pods, or they swim with the boat, but not the swimmers. You can never really predict these things.

I hadn't really planned on being in Hawaii on my birthday. After all, I had already been here earlier this year, in February, leading another dolphin workshop. But then my friends Doug and Trish, whom I was working with that year, asked me to look at coming in May as well. So we announced it, and promoted it, and voila! We had enough attendees to hold a class!

It was smaller than my usual class size, so we opened our boat to other dolphin enthusiasts who might call for an excursion with Captain Veto, owner and skipper of the chartered boat that would take us out to sea. Veto picked up a few "extras." These individuals knew nothing of my work or dolphin communication and were just going out on the boat for the chance to swim with dolphins.

Near the end of our swim, late in the morning, a very large dolphin pod came and swam with us. I was so eager and happy to be with them. When they choose to swim with you, they sometimes make a large loop and circle around at a slower speed. You can usually keep up with them at this pace.

One of the "extras," a woman from our boat who was not part of my group, was swimming near me as I was happily swimming with the dolphins. They were getting ready to leave. You can tell when dolphins are done playing with you because they start to speed up as they get ready to take off. Naturally, I tried to swim faster to keep up with them, and telepathically thought to them, "Oh, please, just one more round with us!"

As I tried to swim faster, my bathing suit, a bandeau strapless style, kept filling with water in the bra area and creating a bit of a drag. So I spontaneously pushed my suit to my waist to ease my swimming. The dolphins "heard" my request and came back! When we got back on the boat the "extra" woman who was near me said, "I noticed the dolphins came back when you showed them your breasts!!!"

My life hasn't always been like that. Seven years ago, when I was 43, my life fell apart. I thought I was half of a happily married couple. We were a family that had been through some pretty rough times personally and professionally and had emerged out from the other side to carve out a new life.

Back in 1993 I was working as the CEO of a Convention and Visitors Bureau and was happily married. I had worked hard to get to this achievement. My husband's job required a long commute. Although he absolutely loved the job he hated the three-hour commute. I was worried because he was so unhappy. We talked about my leaving my job and following him, but he didn't want me to give up this achievement.

I was a big risk taker, and got into a political battle with my board, so they decided I was expendable. Now that my three-year contract was voided, it freed me up to relocate our family to the city in which my husband worked.

Finally we would be in the same city again! I interviewed for my dream job and got it! Our new joint income was substantial. We had managed to stay happily married. I really didn't realize that I was sitting on a time bomb.

Back then, I was so happy, thinking we were finally in a place of deep personal satisfaction. But that was only true for me. I didn't realize that my husband wasn't happy. I guess I was so busy being the optimist that I didn't see the handwriting on the wall. Three months later our life fell apart. My husband of 22 years was asking for a divorce! Our four sons were between the ages of 10 and 18.

This was a crazy time of roller coaster emotions and upheaval. The next twenty-four months contained the sum of the most dramatic changes of lifestyle anyone could imagine. I tried to maintain equilibrium amidst losing my "dream" job and trying to work things out with my husband, but we eventually separated twelve months later.

Concurrently, my husband filed bankruptcy, naming me as one of his creditors *before* our divorce was final. This meant that I became responsible for 100% of our marital debts.

Donald Trump tells the story of being on a date with a woman and walking past a homeless man. He pondered to himself, "I wonder if she is dating me for my money? That homeless man is worth more than me! He may have a net worth of zero, but mine is a negative number!" I knew how that felt! Not only did I start my new life with a negative number, but I was unemployed, had no resources, no credit, and had taken on our joint debt!

Since I had always been able to find a job, and had been interviewing nationally, I figured I would get offered a job in a new city. Knowing that it was very likely I would need to move, I decided to make a deal with my former husband.

I wanted to be able to move anywhere in the country without having to consult him, and he wanted minimal child support payments. I ended up with the child support equivalent for one child—while I had four teenage sons in the house. Well, I figured it was only money, and I was tired of fighting. I wanted my life back. I knew I could always make more money.

The divorce was final a year after our separation, and three years from when the crazy time started. That same summer, our second son was accepted at an Ivy League school. With his grants and loans, the parental obligation towards his tuition was still $10,000 annually! Our oldest son told his younger brother, "Quit dreaming, there is no way that Mom can afford to send you there." At this point, the older one was still depressed about the divorce and had no plans for college.

Fortunately, the younger one's clear intention to attend college inspired his older brother to attend college as well. There is not much sibling rivalry among these two, but knowing his younger brother was attending college did inspire the older one, and helped him move out of his depression.

In the years between my first workshop facilitation and the writing of this book—a time I consider *Genie's* incubation—one of my biggest challenges was to come up with the extra $10,000 a year in cash required for my second son's college tuition. My former husband had no interest in helping our sons with their tuition and was mystified that I would even consider paying this bill. He also was certain that I expected our son to pay me back some day!

I was still unemployed and interviewing locally and nationally. I was offered three different jobs locally, all at half my former income. I decided the Universe had something in mind for me, and that I should pay attention, so I accepted one of the $35,000 a year jobs.

I stayed with that job for the next four years. When the letter from my son's college arrived with the message to make installments of $1,000 a month for the next ten months, I laughed out loud! If I sent them that amount of money, I wouldn't be able to make the house payment! So, I tossed it. No point in letting that scare me!

Finally, I wrote his first semester tuition check for $5,000. I was mentally exhausted! How could I manifest $5,000 seven more times? I knew that the thought of manifesting $40,000, or $10,000 a year over the course of three and a half more years, frightened me so much that I couldn't imagine it!

What did I really want? I sincerely desired for my son to complete his four years of college and graduate! I knew I didn't have to worry about his mental ability or persistence in the classroom. My only concern was my ability to provide the tuition payment before the end of each semester in order for him to register for the following semester.

I pondered this and came up with an idea. On my desk at work I placed a picture of him in cap and gown from high school graduation. Every time I felt afraid —sometimes that was as many as 40 times a day—I would look at that picture and imagine a conversation in the future that went like this, "There were some scary moments, but it really wasn't that hard!" That was my first "movie." The movies became more sophisticated as time went on, but this was essentially the core.

My second son completed his four years at his college, and I paid his tuition each semester. Yes, there were some crazy moments, but it really wasn't that hard. There were amazing opportunities that allowed me to manifest big chunks of money to write those checks.

One semester was especially crazy. I had not paid the tuition from the prior semester, so when he went back to school he couldn't register, because no college will let you take additional classes without paying your prior semester's bill. Some people would admit defeat at this point, but I was determined and he trusted me. He still showed up and attended classes while waiting for the money to materialize! Talk about faith!

Finally I was able to write the check, and he signed up for classes three weeks into the semester! It was a huge hassle to sign up late because most of the professors didn't realize that he had been attending class all along! He never wanted to do that again!

Right before he left for college the very first year, I had a dream. In the dream, he never finished college. I was so upset from that dream that I made him promise me he would finish. He assured me that he was making way too big an investment in time and effort *not* to finish. I believed him and forgot about the dream.

My manifestation movie included my attending his graduation ceremony. Did you know that some students are able to go through graduation ceremonies without having completed the required coursework, so long as they are really close? They just don't receive their diploma yet.

My son still hasn't earned that diploma, even though he maintained honor roll status and was listed as a graduating student with honors in the graduation program! (After being accepted for graduation, closer review caused him to be denied due to one "essential" credit.) This taught me that your movies will have to include all the important details—like seeing a diploma! He and the entire family attended graduation anyway!

I was satisfied that I did my part and have no regrets, although I learned something important here. Who knows why I didn't see the diploma in my movie. Maybe that part was his free will. The main thing is that I succeeded in paying for his education.

v

He has a great job with an international software company that pays very well. He is recognized for his education, as if he had graduated, even though he doesn't have that degree. And he is highly regarded by his employers. But, son, if you are reading this, I would really like you to finish, and so would your wife!

During this challenging time I worked as a fundraiser for a local charity. At my company there was a constant churn of really good support people. This was typical of any non-profit agency, where the wages are low and the workload high. I was told many times, by both my peers and my boss in my agency, that it would be difficult to find an administrative assistant to do everything I wanted with the budget they were allowing me for that purpose.

Using the *Genie System*, I was able to achieve my goal by making a movie that expressed my belief that our organization had something my prospective assistant would desire. I believed that I could find someone who would feel we had things they could not get elsewhere, like good benefits and flexible scheduling that could be traded for wages. The movie focused on how happy both my new assistant and I would be with our mutually beneficial situation. Each time we hired, we always hired fabulous support staff, in spite of the low pay constraint.

In this job, for the first time in a long time, I wasn't the leader of an organization. As a CEO you can easily spend 60-80 hours a week on your job. This new job didn't require that level of commitment, so it became possible for me to pursue my personal interests more deeply.

Due to their long history in the community, my company had a wonderful benefits package that enabled me to earn and take a lot of vacation time. It was a good tradeoff for the low pay. I never took a real vacation during the four years I worked for them.

Instead, I used all of my vacation time traveling on Fridays to workshops all over the USA. This enabled me to pursue a hobby and get certified as a facilitator of a workshop that was starting to gain national recognition.

Within a few years, I was traveling to present this workshop to small groups. Once again, I was using my manifesting skills to create an opportunity to grow and develop a little seminar business. This business grew into having a national clientele of individuals. I continued to work full time during the week and travel to lead seminars on the weekend for the next five years.

At one point in my career, while working in tourism and attempting to educate the community about the local attractions, I decided a local TV show would be an ideal forum. I approached the local public TV station and presented my case for a tourism show. Another individual who was interested in production had been looking for an opportunity to create a show, and the TV station put us together. Thus began my first TV show.

I found I had a knack for television and have hosted a local TV show in each of the three cities I have lived in since 1992. My mother says that is my true calling. My first TV show became so popular that it aired every day for the remaining three years I was in that job. In addition, the largest radio station in the city picked it up and aired the audio portion every week as their public service show. The first two shows were tourism based, because I was head of the tourism bureaus in those two cities.

I hosted *Viewpoints* in Madison, Wisconsin for about a year. Initially they featured me as a guest. I mentioned to the producer that I had hosted a TV show in other cities. Pretty soon I was hosting for them whenever I was in town. Because they liked working with me so much, I became a permanent host and we started taping two and three shows at a time, until my travel schedule made it impossible.

Viewpoints was about alternative subjects from different kinds of healing modalities and energy work to particle physics. Scientists from the University of Wisconsin have gone on the air to talk about neutrinos.[1] We have had medical doctors; lawyers and scientists telling us about successful innovations that have helped people heal and improve their lives. It is an exciting format we hoped would go national some day. They continued to air the shows for a year after I left.

---

[1] I had never heard of neutrinos until I interviewed these scientists. Neutrinos are subatomic particles that physicists are learning about by tracking their movements. Our guest, a graduate student, had just returned from the South Pole tracking station.

The *Genie* first shows itself

What I really wanted to do was write a book. But that was too far out for me to imagine, so I decided that the only way to create a book on the process that I had developed was to do something really dramatic and relatively straightforward that would lead to the book writing itself.

I kept wondering what I would call this method, and ran one of my first *Genie* movies where someone was thanking me for writing the book. Spontaneously, I called it by name in the first visualization that became a movie-of-the-mind. That movie provided the spontaneous conversation where I called it "Genie in the Bottle!"

Even though writing a book was my heart's desire, I had no idea where to begin. The workshop idea kept returning. If I created a workshop with all the information I was putting together, the book would just show up! For me, it would be easier to lead a workshop than to write a book.

My trade association has an annual meeting that I thought I could present to. I also figured that if I could get named as a speaker on their roster, it would prove that the *Genie* material was perfect for manifesting even the most unusual ideas.

Getting selected to speak seemed daunting. In fact, in hindsight, it was a pretty daring idea to think that a woman who had no credentials and no degree would be named a speaker! I just followed the principles and tools I developed for the *Genie System* and the rest is magic.

I also surmised that if I got the speaking engagement, somehow the material for the workshop would come to me in a format that would lead to writing this book! I started out with the concept that I would present to the National Society of Fund Raising Executives at their national association meeting. Five thousand people usually attend.

If you have ever been to a national association meeting, the breakout sessions are like bar hopping. It is commonplace for a conference attendee to skip around to different breakout sessions, and no one takes the coming and going personally. You select several sessions that you find interesting, knowing you cannot attend all of them. If the first one doesn't excite you, you try another.

My goal was to present such a riveting session that no one would leave, all the seats would be taken, and there would be standing room only! Within 12 months of creating this goal I accomplished it, and repeated it the following year.

For my speaking in the breakout sessions, I created a movie where no one left, and more and more people kept coming into the room. My movie came true! No one left the room! We had standing room only.

How did I get on the roster in the first place? I ran into an old friend who was leaving the fundraising field. I shared what was going on in my life. Spontaneously, I told her about my desire to be a presenter at this association meeting. After all, she was leaving and wouldn't be in competition with me.

Amazingly, she provided me with details on how to submit a proposal, which was due in three weeks, and added, "If you submit it for this year, I will speak in favor of it, because I sit on the committee!" She was the one person who would be strongly in favor of this sort of workshop on the committee. She believed there was not enough self-development coursework and she felt the *Genie* workshop would address that!

She was the exact person to help me and presented herself to me with little or no effort on my part. Coincidence? I think not, we almost didn't meet! The only thing I did was run my movie over and over in my head and then respond to the opportunity to meet with the perfect person to aid me in my goal.

Of course, I had to do my part. I had to prepare an outline to submit to the committee, which had to be substantial enough to get to the committee review in the first place!

This accomplishment was so huge for me that the first year I was almost in a daze that I actually pulled it off! The second year was the test of my true mettle; for I could see clearly what I had accomplished and wondered if I could do it again. Certainly if it was a coincidence, the odds were against me! If I could do it again, it proved the *Genie System* worked. It did.

During this cycle of four years, while working at the non-profit organization, I was running a lot of movies. I wanted to have my bills paid off. I wanted to be a great mom and parent. I wanted to do an awesome job at my day job. I wanted to succeed at the seminar business I was starting. I wanted lots of things.

I began offering tours to Egypt during this period. When I was in Egypt, the people called me Mrs. Magic, because many magical things happened while I was there with my groups.

When everyone else was discontinuing trips to Egypt, I was bringing people. I found that when I worked with this magical formula, I was much more plugged into life and how things work than I could ever have imagined. The *Genie* material will really help you gain this mastery, but more importantly, it will help you define and create your heart's desire, just like magic.

My life is far from perfect. I have many challenges every day. Sometimes I forget to make a movie. Sometimes I stew over the things I don't want. I have found that an attitude of gratitude disperses resistance, and that what I dwell on has a way of returning again and again.

I have learned that I can "Be a Genie," and you can be too. I am so grateful to the participants of my workshops, to my editor and publisher and all my supporters for the opportunity to share what I have learned and discovered. I know that if you learn and apply the information contained in this book, **you** will "Be a Genie."

Update 2013

The original version of this book, *You are the Genie in the Bottle*, was written back in 1994 and was first released in manuscript form. It was written with *The Principles & Proofs* first and *The Practices* second. It was my firm belief that the reader needed to understand "why" this material is so profound before they applied the practices. Now, many years later, I've changed my mind and have concluded you can get into the practices first. Learn what is possible before you completely understand the proven principles. You'll have a chance to get some solid experiences and successes with it, followed by learning the scientific principles that will give you the know-how and understanding of why this works.

After you've read the practices, please keep going. I urge you to continue to read all the principles and proofs, too. They will give you the foundation and staying power you need to produce your heart's desires. With a few successes under your belt, you'll come back over and over to the sacred geometry found in the *Genie System*. Learning the Phoenix Sequence will change the way you think – and you'll thank me later. In fact, my files are filled with grateful client letters who took the course in those early years, learning the sacred geometry right along with the practices. That's why this book is so different!

For those who have the need to know and understand the proven scientific principles that support the *Genie System*, you may wish to read the chapters in Part II first. If you are anxious to get started learning "how" to use the *Genie System*, go ahead and start with Part I. Either order is acceptable. You may wish to think of Part I as **your** instruction manual and Part II as **God's** owner manual.

It is my desire that you will grant me the authority to teach you, and as you learn your lessons through our shared experiences along with your own personal practice, you will gain the mastery I have gained without all of the trial and error!

Although this book was received through intuition, I have made every effort to back up my assertions with sources that confirm what I was led to know. I hope you appreciate my deep pleasure in discovering that this information can be supported by logical, scientific argument.

This book is intended to teach you all that I have learned about creating your heart's desire and manifesting, so you, too, can "Be a Genie." I welcome your stories and insights.

Maureen J. St. Germain, January 2003, Naples, FL, and May 2003, Cairo, Egypt, and October 2013, New York, NY

Part I

The Practices

Chapter 1

The Five Steps

Introduction

How would you like to create the life you want? Live your dreams? Get more enjoyment out of life and relationships? Much of *Be a Genie* is based on technical information. Yet it is presented in a way that will be simple, straightforward and easy to understand. In the first part of this book you will find innovative practices that will help you achieve your dreams. You will discover in *Genie* that you have a step-by-step explanation so that your rational mind can accept what the intuitive part of you already knows: you are the creator of your reality.

In Part I of this book, *The Practices*, you will learn how to use the *Genie System* for manifestation. Part II, *The Principles & Proofs*, presents the basic scientific principles of manifestation. Although *The Practices* introduces the *Genie System*, you will find that the chapters of *The Principles & Proofs* present the scientific foundation of the *Genie System* supported by the important underlying mathematical and scientific principles of all creation.

Utilizing this material will seem like child's play once you get the hang of it. A wonderful side effect of this work is the empowerment you will feel. You will develop personal strengths and experience a connection with Creative Forces that will make your life seem like magic.

Your life will appear to be magical because you will be in the rhythm and flow of the game of life. You will no longer be an outsider wishing to join in, and then getting pulled in by surprise. The Universe expects you to join in the game by giving you synchronicity to tell you that you are in the right game. The *Genie System* teaches you to understand the rules!

If you knew that you could follow a treasure map to easily manifest your heart's desire would you hesitate to use it? Hardly. The *Genie System* is one such treasure map. Once you understand the principles of sacred geometry and apply them using the tools provided, you will discover a world of manifestation awaits you. Enjoy the journey. It is a fabulous ride.

The Universe is waiting for you to do your part. The *Genie System* is intended to provide clarity so that you can see your part in the creation that already exists, and to show you how you can join in the creative process. The *Genie* material enables you to see your role clearly enough to differentiate between the Universe's and your part.

Once you clearly understand, your part the application is simple. The *Genie System* is like a treasure map to follow. When you fully integrate this knowledge and start to apply it to your manifestations, you will be creating in harmony with the Universe. Understanding and applying the map's guidance and information will lead to you discovering that you, too, can "Be a Genie."

Sold out concert tickets

The following true story shows the five steps in action. It involved the son of Rhonda,[2] who had learned manifestation techniques at a workshop I had given. Rhonda's son, Jason, age 12, really wanted to attend a rock concert that was being held near Chicago, at a rock concert stage called Alpine Valley that was about 40 miles from their home in Madison.

Jason's parents had the means to pay for the ticket to the concert, so money wasn't the issue. But like most concerts of this type, within an hour of the tickets going on sale they were sold out, even though the concert was some six weeks out. Jason's mom had done her part, and had been on the phone for the entire hour trying to get through, to no avail. She felt badly, knowing Jason's passion for this rock band, but felt there was nothing she could do. Like most moms she would have done anything within her means to help her son get what he wanted, including attending a rock concert with him.

---

[2] Names have been changed for the privacy of the individuals.

Jason knew his mom had an interest in manifesting and asked her, "Can't you do something Mom?" Wanting her son to be really clear about his request, she asked him "Like what?" He said, "You know, that stuff you do... his voice trailing off..." Rhonda knew what he meant, and said, "All right but *you* have to do it, I can only teach you *how* to do it, I cannot do it for you." She remembered well what she had learned in class. And it's true: we can only make our *own* magic.

So Rhonda told Jason to visualize *being at the concert*. This part is important. He had to see himself in the outcome. The next part was more difficult for Jason. He announced to his friends at school that he was going to go to the rock concert. (I don't recommend this. Why accept all that "feedback" to discard it later?) His friends all laughed at him. His mother, Rhonda, encouraged him to keep seeing himself at the concert, and feeling the feeling (excitement, joy, fun, etc.) and to ignore the feedback from his friends that didn't serve him.

A few days later, they heard about the concert on the radio. A local radio station was giving away tickets to the concert. The radio station would be using one of the local bars they frequently used for such drawings. The drawing would happen on the day of the concert.

Jason and his mom showed up early at the bar. The bartenders said, "No there wasn't going to be a give-away today." (More negative feedback to disregard.) They decided to "hang out" anyway. Within the hour, two of the DJ's from the radio station showed up, and said they had forgotten to call the bar to let them know they were coming to do this give-away tonight. They had three pairs of tickets to give away for this concert.

At this point, Jason got pretty excited and told his mom that he hoped he would win the tickets. Recognizing that one could hold tickets and still not be at the concert, Rhonda corrected him and said, "Don't worry about winning the tickets, just see yourself at the concert. If you were already at the concert, what would that feel like?"

By now the bar was getting pretty filled up with people who had hoped to win tickets. There wasn't a lot of time for the hour's drive to Alpine Valley, where the band would be performing. The drawing was held. All three pairs were given away. Jason didn't win. He was so incredulous.

How could this be? His mom told him he did everything right. Just then, one of the winners came up to Jason. She handed the tickets to him and said, "I'd like you to have these, they [the band] obviously mean a lot more to you than to me."

The seats were center stage, five rows up from the stage. Jason was ecstatic. Rhonda said, "Your friends will never believe you. You should take the ticket stubs to school tomorrow, to prove you were there."

Jason accomplished his outcome through the ever-changing dynamic of the reality because he kept putting his outcome back into the equation. Every time feedback, in the form of a circumstance or a person, challenged the validity of his belief, he recycled *his* outcome into the equation. Surprisingly, Jason put additional obstacles in his own path (such as telling his friends he was going to attend the concert before actually getting tickets) to prove just how very skilled he could be. I believe that the Universe folded in upon itself to create the reality that he held, because he continued to input his own feedback in spite of some pretty impressive obstacles.

More sold out concert tickets

This is not the only case of someone who was able to get concert tickets for a sold-out performance. Jeanette wanted to go to a concert in Madison that was sold out before she could get tickets. At first she was so disappointed, but then remembered the story of Jason from the *Genie* class, and decided "NO!" She wasn't going to give up that easily. She understood the scientific principles employed in the *Genie System* and did everything outlined in this book. She used the five steps, ran her movie, and held a clear outcome.

Her daughter's boyfriend overheard his co-workers talking about this same performing group. One of them had a part-time job where the concert was taking place. She said that the company sponsoring the event had not used all the tickets they had reserved and were returning the extra ones to the box office.

When her daughter's boyfriend called Jeanette's daughter, wondering if her mom still wanted to see this performer, both Jeanette and her daughter were surprised that her boyfriend had even remembered her interest in them since he had only heard about it once.

Jeanette acted quickly and was able to purchase wonderful seats and attend the concert of her heart's desire! Her manifestation work enabled her to hear about tickets opening up in time to act. Her clear visual image of seeing herself at the concert made it possible for her to get the "clear channel" of information in a way that facilitated her to take advantage of it. In the *Genie* work, opportunities such as this seem to come out of thin air.

The five steps of *Genie* manifestation and your picture of reality

The Universe conforms to your picture of reality. What you think about is what you will manifest, even if your thoughts are subconscious. You do that now. You have your unique viewpoint. No one sees the world quite like you do. Do you want to manifest by default or design?

Generally, individuals subscribe to a widely-held view of the reality from which manifestations are created. You can step out of the limitations of "collective reality" anytime you want. Every day you make choices for yourself that puts the Universe into motion for you.

Do you want to manifest by default or design?

Noted futurist, Gerald Celente[3] states, "The people have to will it [the changes] as well. I believe we *do* will our future. If we live individually – living in terms of hate, power, control and fear – then that's the lives we are going to live individually. If individually we think about love compassion, kindness – contact with the Gods – whatever Gods may mean to you, then that is the kind of life we are going to live. Just as we do

---

[3] Celente, Gerald, futurist, owner of Trends Institute in an interview with George Noory on *Coast to Coast AM* radio show July 15, 2003. He was speaking of a new 'Global Age' where we may be able to create a renaissance in spirituality, art, science, literature and intellectual thought. Celente is the same man who in the early 70's and 80's predicted the major trend in gourmet coffee. Starbucks, the leader in this trend, had only seventeen shops in 1992. Celente is author of numerous books including *Trend Tracking* and *Trends 2000*.

individually, we will do it collectively. I think if people will a change, change will happen."

The five steps are designed to assist you in understanding how to create change. Once you understand these steps, applying them will become as natural as driving a car. Like driver's education classes, this book is filled with new methods to avoid crashes, ways to drive in difficult weather, advice on how to read road signs, and tips from experienced drivers.

The five steps are:

1. Understand and integrate the science—sacred geometry, the creation process, quantum mechanics and chaos theory. Use your logic and intuition equally.
2. Make sure your desire is strong and your belief real.
3. Fill your heart's desire with your emotion.
4. Allow your feelings to show you what happens next.
5. Make a movie about your desired outcome and run it frequently, especially when you need to build your confidence.

One – understanding the science

Chapters 11 through 17 ("Part II - The Principles & Proofs") detail the scientific principles needed for *Genie* manifestation. You may experience some resistance from your rational mind which wants to control things, because it thinks it has done a pretty good job of managing your affairs up until now, so why shouldn't it continue?

Once you understand and integrate these principles, your thought process will be more open to both thinking and experiencing "outside the box." You will begin accepting imagination and intuition as aids in manifestation. Your awareness is more than the sum total of your thoughts.

Typically you use the left side of your brain for all the logical thoughts you think. The right side, the artistic and intuitive side, is active but usually it can't get information to you in an understandable manner in order to make use of all of the information that has been collected.

Because the intuitive side collects data in a unique, non-logical way, it can read aspects of individual's behaviors and information in the reality that your logical side cannot collect or interpret. Science is still discovering how this works. However, you may have had experiences that have opened your awareness to this kind of "knowing."

How many times have you "sensed" something about a situation, yet failed to act because your logic didn't support it? Very often, when you have no vehicle to translate sensing, you tend to ignore it. You need both kinds of information to know the whole picture. The balance between logic and intuition creates this balance.

You can support this process of using both sides of your brain by writing or drawing with your left hand, using left brain-right brain sensory type books like "Magic Eye," or listening to music created for the purpose of re-uniting the left and right brain.[4] Using these materials will enhance your ability to see and react to opportunities that come your way.

Two – desire and belief

Deciding what it is that you really want is essential. Make your manifestations something so important that all other things will seem small and unimportant beside it. Make it something so urgent that you can say to yourself, "this is who I am, and I must have it, be it, become it." It is possible to manifest without this deep passion, if you are capable of fully focusing on your heart's desire, but passion will give you the staying power and determination you will need to go the long haul.

The stronger your personal belief system, the stronger your ability to manifest your own reality. It is very important to be clear with your desire. The following story helps to illustrate the passion you will need to be clear with the Universe.

Mac Anderson-Whitehurst, a locksmith I know in Greensboro, NC, never charges for unlocking a car if there is a child being rescued from it. He has been known to show up within ten minutes for a desperate parent when in

---

[4] The Monroe Institute has wonderful programs and CDs that will enhance the left brain-right brain experience. Their popular CD series can be obtained through www.metamusic.com.

normal traffic the trip should take twenty minutes. His policy is "No charge." He figures that a parent is already stressed out enough about their child being locked in a car.

This man has no children of his own and regards everyone's children as priceless. He believes that parents shouldn't be charged for a service call when they are already upset and concerned about a child's welfare. However, every once in a while, a parent calls and wants to know "How much will it cost to unlock a car with a child in it?" In those cases, he does charge.

His policy is that if a parent has an approach of "no price is too high" to keep their child safe, then they get his full support. If the parent has to ask the price of getting a locked child out of their car, what does that say about their priorities? What does it say about the value they place on their child? Isn't every child priceless and irreplaceable?

Isn't your *baby*, your heart's desire, the most important thing in your world as you nurture and grow it into maturity?

Believing in yourself

Consider giving yourself permission to believe in yourself. It is not necessary that you believe in yourself, but it certainly helps your *Genie* work. Individuals can manifest things even though they really don't believe in themselves all the time. Because they understand the scientific basis and practiced the steps, they were able to manifest in spite of their self-doubt.

Farmers expend a huge amount of money to generate income, and it is always a gamble. My father, a greenhouse farmer, invested $100,000 on his spring crop before receiving any results. He spent the same amount on his fall crop, too. This was in 1965, when $200,000 went a lot further than it does today. The money was used for seed, wages, heating the greenhouse, fertilizer, and general overhead expenses that all businesses incur.

As you start to think of the next thing you will manifest, you need to commit yourself to the time, energy, and probably a cash investment. Think of your heart's desire as a plant that you are growing from seed.

You wouldn't consider pulling out the shoots to see if they were growing. You know you have to give the seeds time to grow, and MATURE.

When you start to worry that your latest manifestation isn't bearing any fruit, remember that produce takes a season, and your creation takes its season also. Be patient. Remember, holding your outcome firmly in mind is the SINGLE most important thing you can do for yourself. Be like the farmer: plant seeds, water, and wait. Expect a bountiful harvest. And ask for a benevolent outcome.

Three – adding emotions

The emotions that you will want to access to enhance your movie are love, gratitude and joy. Emotions are the rocket fuel of manifesting. When you add your emotions to the movie you are making, you give your manifestations a jump-start. If you don't imbue your movies with emotion it will be more difficult to create.

It is so important that you learn to use your heart to connect with that universal flow of love, joy and gratitude. Focus on feeling these feelings. When you do, you will begin to experience such energetic support that you will never have to worry about lack. You will always feel that there is enough.

You will begin to understand and feel that you are in an abundant flow that allows you to take and give as much as you want. Your feelings of love, gratitude and joy create emotional resonance that attracts experiences that cause you to have more of those same emotions. Like attracts like.

> *Work like you don't need the money.*
> *Love like you'll never get hurt.*
> *Dance like nobody's watching.*
>
> - Satchel Paige, First African American
> to pitch in a Major League World Series

Figure 1-1

Using emotional resonance

If you have really created your heart's desire, you will be able to experience gratitude. When you learn to nurture an attitude of gratitude you are starting to experience your heart's desire as a real thing. When you vibrate at a particular emotional frequency, you create a field of resonance.

The feelings you create with the emotion from your heart serve as a homing device into the quantum field creating your new present moment. These feelings are emotional resonance. This field will draw more of the same to you. This is explained in further detail in Chapter 8, "Resistance, Resonance and Feedback."

Lessons from aerodynamics

By using the mind and emotions, the physical body creates a magnetic resonance strong enough to affect physical matter.[5] Make your resonance a strong and heartfelt one of joy and gratitude.

Your attitude is like your altitude. The fuller your emotion of joy and gratitude the higher you can fly. Your altitude is your capacity to contain self-esteem.

If you were to study the principles of aerodynamics, one of the first lessons you learn is how planes get their lift. While the air under the wings helps give the plane lift when it is getting off the ground, it is actually the air traveling **over** the curved **wing** that creates negative pressure which gives the plane its lift. The air beneath the plane has to move faster to go around it, and thus creates this uplift. Use your emotion, i.e. your homing device, to "provide lift" into a point in the quantum field.

The level from which we operate is the applied altitude. Your attitude resides in the grid created by your ethics and principles. I call this your *personal* matrix. Everyone has one. This personal matrix is like the kind of

---

[5] Talbot, Michael, *The Holographic Universe*, HarperCollins, 1991, page 5. "...in 1987, physicist Robert G. Jahn, and clinical psychologist Brenda J. Dunne, both at Princeton University, announced that after a decade of rigorous experimentation by their Princeton Engineering Anomalies Research Laboratory, they had accumulated unequivocal evidence that the mind can psychically interact with the physical reality."

equipment you purchase. As you become more sophisticated, you begin to demand a more advanced level of equipment. (Chapter 2, "The Matrix", is full of information on your matrix and how to create and maintain it.)

Learn to practice an attitude of gratitude

How is it possible for you to be grateful for something that doesn't exist? Think about the last time you were really, really grateful for something that pleased you. Let your feeling of gratitude evolve into gratitude for your new outcome. The Universe keeps returning to you what you send out. So make sure you send out gratitude. The rewards will stack up.

Your attitude of gratitude disperses resistance. You can always find some specific thing to be grateful for. Perhaps you can be grateful for the clarity of discovering what it is you do *not* desire. Or perhaps you can be grateful for some other aspect of the outcome, such as something that you learned about yourself.

Four – using emotion to create what happens next

Next you will create a visual image of your desired outcome. What does that look like, what does it feel like? How will your life be different now that you have this "desired outcome"? Allow the feelings to fill every part of you. Perhaps in the past you stopped the visualization at this point, before seeing what happens next.

In the *Genie* work, you will go *beyond* the place of achieving your heart's desire. Your job includes seeing something tangible that is proof positive that you have already achieved your outcome in the future. What you are learning to see and feel is the reality *after* your heart's desire has been achieved. As those feelings fill you, ask yourself, "What happens next?" Base it on all possibilities – all choices.

What happens next?

Your job is to imagine a place where you have already achieved your heart's desire and are looking backwards from there at your achievement. From that vantage point you already *have* your heart's desire. After visualizing "what happens next," personalize your outcome with a one-on-one conversation. If you have truly imagined your manifestation as being

11

in the present moment, you will then be able to feel what happens next effortlessly.

Purposefully bring into the movie someone who is important to you, who will share your enthusiasm when you re-visit achieving your heart's desire. This conversation must occur in your movie. This one-on-one conversation is key.

The conversation could be with a friend or a stranger. It could be in person or over the phone. The conversation is personal, and you allow it to percolate up from your subconscious. If you don't know who the person is, make it someone who would be likely to be in your reality if your heart's desire had already been achieved.

How can it be someone you don't know? If you see yourself as a performer it could be a fan, if you see yourself with your as yet unmet beloved, then the conversation might be with him or her.

For example, if you have been yearning for a new car, first see yourself in the experience of driving it. This car you are driving fulfills your desire for a new car. What does that *feel* like?

You can visualize a specific make and model, but the fastest and easiest way to manifest something like a car is to focus on your *feelings*. Focus on the *feeling of driving and owning* a car that fulfills your needs, then see yourself having a conversation with someone you know. This dialog might involve them noticing you driving your new car. Then, leave the rest of the details to the Universe.

Five – make your movie

From your visualization, a movie emerges based upon the feelings and conversation you've held. This is where you evoke the feelings that come from knowing you have achieved your heart's desire and are ready for what comes next. This next event is what your conversation is about.

You prepare for your movie debut by visualizing the outcome that you desire and continuing it to an event that occurs after you have achieved that outcome. The first scene in your *Genie* movie is the "after" event (Figure 1-2).

12

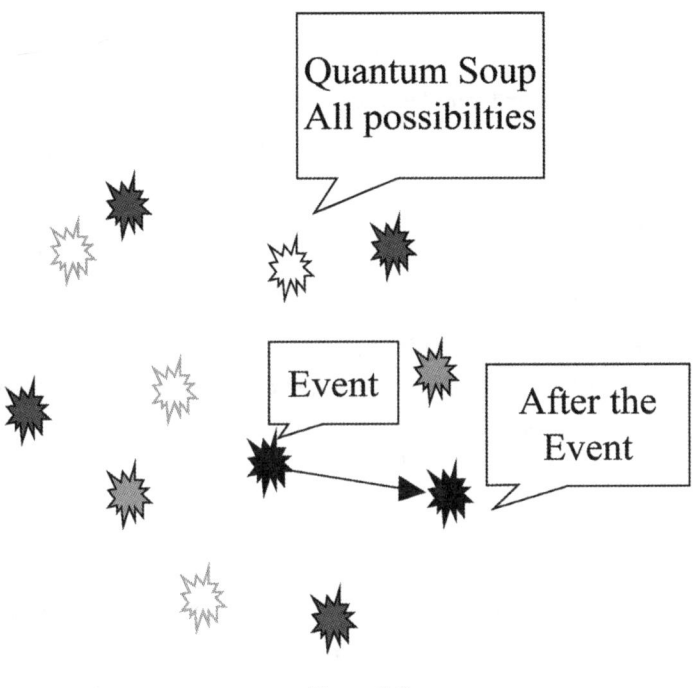

Figure 1-2

For example, you might desire to be happily married. The event after the event might be an anniversary celebration. Your movie's opening scene is the anniversary party reflecting on the events that have led to this moment. The movie includes a present time conversation you are having at this anniversary party.

The first time you run your movie, you may be surprised by the conversation's direction. Every time you run your movie, you should go to the deepest level of emotion you can achieve.

Running your movie takes only a few moments—and it can put a smile on your face no matter what else is happening in your life. You can repeat your movie as often as you like. Each time you run it you are creating resonance and thus increasing the probability that the events will actually occur.

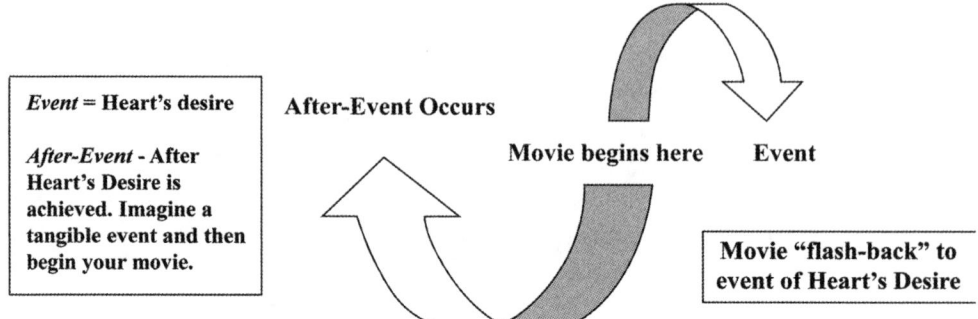

Event = Heart's desire	After-Event Occurs
After-Event - After Heart's Desire is achieved. Imagine a tangible event and then begin your movie.	Movie begins here Event
	Movie "flash-back" to event of Heart's Desire

Your movie begins after you have achieved the "after-event".
Then you flashback to the event that is your "heart's desire".
Allow yourself to see what happens next.

Figure 1-3

Summary

The five steps provide you with the practical template to manifest your heart's desire. You are the CEO of your own personal corporation. Your "employee" is the Universe. Of course you hire really wonderful employees (i.e. THE UNIVERSE) who understand how to carry out your wishes perfectly.

Make sure you have a good understanding of sacred geometry, quantum mechanics and chaos theory. This knowledge supports the use of your whole brain. It empowers you to use both logic and intuition equally (Explained in "Part II - The Principles & Proofs").

The intuitive side of your brain is able to gather a kind of data that defies traditional logic and supports your "suspending disbelief" in order to create and run your movie in the quantum zone.

Find the outcome that looks and feels like having your heart's desire. Give yourself permission to have the ideal result. Focus on how you would feel to have your heart's desire.

Your job is to focus on *what* you want, not *how* to get it. The "how it will occur" will be shown to you. Any actions you need to take will present themselves, usually in a manner that seems spontaneous, easy or

14

coincidental. Action steps from the Universe come in a very gentle manner.

The fifth step describes how to make a movie that goes beyond your outcome, to a place where you see your heart's desire as having happened in the past. You experience the event *after* your outcome with the emotions of love, gratitude or joy. Personalize this experience with a one-on-one conversation in your mind. When you run your movie, it automatically creates the circumstances that will *pull your outcome to you.*

Learn the principles of "The Phoenix Factor" covered in Chapter 14, "Introducing Fibonacci and the Phoenix Sequence." The after-event becomes the central point of your imagined place, your *movie-of-the-mind.* This place in the future is experienced in your present as a past event. This after-event ultimately becomes the central theme of the movie you create. This *movie-of-the-mind* contains all the elements we have described above.

Review - The five basic steps to creating your heart's desire:

❖ Understand the science—sacred geometry, the creation process, quantum mechanics and chaos theory.
❖ Make sure your desire is strong and your belief real.
❖ Add the emotions of love, gratitude or joy to your event.
❖ Let your feelings lead you to what happens next and experience a conversation with someone supportive or pertinent to the new outcome.
❖ Start your movie with "after the event" and run it often, especially when you need to boost your confidence.

Chapter 2

The Matrix, Genie Movie and Lighthouse

Gregg Braden writes in his book, *Awakening to Zero Point*, about one of his Egypt tours that had traveled from one police checkpoint to another in Egypt. This trip always takes three hours yet this time they arrived at their destination in one and a half hours.

My first tour group in Egypt duplicated this. When we arrived at our destination an hour and a half early, the owner of Quest Travel greeted us with the following statement, "No one except Gregg Braden has ever done that before!"

The miner who altered time

Deepak Chopra, MD, the well-known healer, tells the story of a group of miners in Germany who were caught in a mine collapse in the 1990s. They were cut off from the rest of the world, and more importantly, from the fresh air. They calculated there was enough oxygen for about three days. Only one miner had a watch. He arbitrarily chose to alter the timekeeping by informing his fellow miners that only one hour had passed for every two hours on his watch.

They were rescued after five days. Only one miner was dead. Who's your guess? It was the timekeeper. Everyone else had believed him, and his version of time keeping.

I wasn't satisfied with this story – so I did the math. I assumed someone else started keeping time after the man with the watch died, and switched back to "planetary time" or "3-D time." Looking at the reality from the outside, the miner with the watch died on day three based on *his* belief system. The remaining miners' belief systems caused them to think that his death occurred on day one and a half. Day four would be the middle of the second day for the miners. Day five is halfway through the miners' day three, within their parameters of "survivable", according to their modified belief systems.

16

Understanding how "belief systems" influence reality

Research into the human sleep-wake cycle bears out the likelihood of the miners losing track of time. In research that was done on jet lag and insomnia, "German researchers found that after some weeks the sleep-wake cycle would detach itself from the temperature cycle and become erratic. People would stay awake for twenty or thirty hours at a time, followed by ten or twenty hours of sleep. Not only would the subjects remain unaware that their day had lengthened, they refused to believe it when told." [6]

The matrix

A matrix is an enclosed environment in which something develops. (It is from the Latin word for womb.) A matrix, as it is used here, is a "safe zone" in which you create your heart's desire. It is the part of the reality that you choose to tune into because it supports your new creation. The matrix will be the location in the quantum zone where all the action of your *Genie* Movie occurs, but it is also the place where both your heart's desire and the after-event occur. In the *Genie System*, the matrix is encased inside the Lighthouse, much like a movie is played in a movie theater.

When you go to the I-MAX or Cinema you "suspend disbelief." You step into a new matrix established by the projection of the movie in the theater. You encounter events you might not experience in your daily life, yet react with horror, fear, joy and laughter as if those events are real. Your *movie-of-the-mind*, your *Genie* Movie, is created using tools found in this book, learning to express your heart's desire through your own matrix, which we call the Lighthouse, and which allows you to *suspend disbelief* about **how** your heart's desire could possibly occur. Not knowing "**how**" your desired outcome will arrive or occur is critical. It allows you to *suspend disbelief* that you could ever have it! Not needing to know how you will achieve your outcome is a necessary element to manifestation!

I was using the term "matrix" back in 1994, long before the *The Matrix*[7] movie came out, but if you have seen it, it will certainly help you

---

[6] Gleick, James, *Chaos,* page 286.
[7] *The Matrix* was first released March 31, 1999.

understand my concept of the matrix. In the original, the matrix was a system of reality maintained by a machine.

In the movie, the matrix controlled everything the humans inside it experienced. Those outside the matrix accessed it by plugging into the machine that was linked into it. I recommend seeing *The Matrix*, because it so clearly conveys the sense of a living matrix, fueled by some outside source. (There is some violence in it – so cover your chakras before watching it by placing your right hand above your crown chakra and then trace it in front of your body – all the way down in front of you, intending that your chakras are now closed. This is similar to a motion you might make to close the eyelids with your hand.)

The matrix operates like an incubator or womb. In visual terms, it is the "work zone" that you have created to contain your movie set and later to run the actual movie of your heart's desire.

Where does the matrix come from?

The matrix comes from your belief system about how the world works. It is the framework, the infrastructure, of the reality. As long as you are in integrity, as you change your beliefs, your matrix changes with you. As your matrix adjusts, so does the world around you. Anything you do in the real world affects the matrix that you experience in the imagined world of your *Genie* Movie. You can strengthen your matrix by acting on your beliefs and desires. You weaken it when you compromise yourself.

As long as you are in integrity, as your beliefs change, your matrix adjusts right along with you!

Imagine for a moment the water supply of a city. When the water is polluted it affects everyone and everything in the system. When your personal integrity is challenged, your matrix is adversely affected, even though **you** may be unaware of that transgression. Your subconscious notes this lack of integrity. This produces distrust in your reality that you may not realize comes directly from your own behavior!

The matrix flows from your own personal sphere of influence – *you* control it. You can create a personal sphere of influence that is so powerful that it overrides all the other spheres of influence. (The next chapter, "Spheres of Influence," covers this in much greater detail.)

The matrix is inescapably linked to your personal sphere, much like the city water supply analogy above. Whatever happens in your world that you don't trust will affect your matrix. Not trusting is like drinking polluted water.

Integrity and trust are two sides of a coin

Remember that integrity and trust are linked. Why? Because often you don't trust in categories of life where you are out of integrity. Notice your behavior. Create a clear awareness of your own integrity – and "trust" (or lack there-of) ceases to be a detracting influence.

Can you drink polluted water and survive? Yes, but once you know the source of your pollution it makes sense to clean it up (i.e. clean up your own out-of-integrity issues). It is possible to manifest in the *Genie System* without perfection? Of course! All of us do it in spite of our mistakes. Just remember that your manifestations improve as your integrity improves. Make a decision to *notice* when you are out of integrity – and watch your manifestations improve as you shift and create balance between your words, thoughts and actions.

A matrix is a conceptual model of a whole system that you create in the void where all possibilities exist. You give it substance with your standards, your ideas, dreams and, most importantly, your feelings. You add life to your manifestation with your observations and emotions. This in turn fuels the incubator you have created in such a way that it is possible to experience what it is really like to have your heart's desire.

Once you complete your *Genie* Movie it continues to live in a different time and space from the one you are experiencing now. It is a living energy field. Your *Genie* Movie emerges from your matrix to exist in a world in which all the stories have the ending you desire.

Once the matrix is fully loaded with your *Genie* Movie, you will use this same energy center (location) to run it. It is as if the movie set transforms into a theater when it is ready to broadcast the finished movie.

Matrix in the *Genie System*

The matrix in the *Genie System* is the "home" of four components. The first component is the background set-up or mood creator. The second is the *Genie* Movie set. The third component is the theater that runs the *Genie* Movie. The final component is the achieving of your heart's desire. You will be using your heart's desire as a past event, which is why it is one of the four components.

First Component – Create the Mood

The *Genie* Movie

When you make your *Genie* Movie, you are not concerned with how or when because *you are in the place where all possibilities exist.* Close your eyes and allow yourself to move into a relaxed state. You do not need to write it out.

You choose one possibility to be the version of the reality that is your heart's desire. This may seem odd at first, but recognize that there can be more than one version of the reality that produces your heart's desire. For example, if you want a new car, does it have to be a Jeep Cherokee? Or could it be any SUV? You have no car payments now, so if you don't want car payments, does it mean you paid cash? Or someone gave it as a gift? You don't care about these details and instead just know your car is paid for without you knowing the "how." All of this goes into your *Genie* Movie of that particular heart's desire. At some point, after you charge up the *Genie* Movie with your joy, happiness and pleasure, it becomes so real that it and the matrix are unified.

Movie elements

Your *Genie* Movie has many elements. Your *movie-of-the-mind* takes place in an ideal future that is not attached to time. Time itself is a construct that gives you a chance to experience the details of an event. You neither know when this will occur nor do you care, unless time is a factor, such as I had when I was manifesting $5,000 per semester that I needed to pay by a specific time for my son's tuition. (Each semester must be paid for before you can enroll in the following one.) You can make

Genie Movies about goals that are related to time specific events, but regardless, each *Genie* Movie is based on some event that happens *after* the desired outcome has already occurred.

When I visualized my son's **paid tuition,** it involved a college graduation. That is *one version.* A different version might have been a paid-in-full letter, or money in the bank, alternate versions that I didn't choose for various reasons. I didn't know *when* I would have that in my real-time "Genie movie-of-the-mind" special conversation where I said to him, "Honey, you know there were some scary moments, but it wasn't that hard." Yet, I did see him wearing a cap and gown during the conversation, so it very likely would be occurring sometime during his graduation ceremony.

Meet the star of the *Genie* Movie

Create *Genie* Movies that will picture your outcome the way you would like it. Your movie's outcome features you as the star, and it should please you very much. If your *Genie* Movie doesn't please you, then keep rewriting the script until it does.

You are the scriptwriter, director and star. What movie star wouldn't jump at the chance to control the script, and direct and star in the movie? Lots of well-known artists do this. You can too! You have *total artistic control.*

Once you start to get into the feeling of creating your outcome and being both director and principle actor in your movie, you will find it very easy to embellish details. It is important that you allow the movie to be spontaneous.

Make it real

The more tangible and realistic your movie is, in your mind, the more closely your actual manifestation will resemble your *Genie* Movie. Research bears this out. Studies have shown that athletes who imagine performing perfectly for a percentage of their practice time achieve the same results as if they had spent all their time practicing.[8]

---

[8] Talbot, Michael, *The Holographic Universe*, p. 88. In an Australian study, three groups of basketball players were compared. As expected, the group that practiced free throws

Experience your heart's desire in its fullest. See and hear the conversation you will have around this. Feel the emotion of it. If you allow the feeling body to fully resonate, you can usually tell when you are in that place: a smile breaks out all over you, your shoulders may drop and you feel warm and fuzzy. It feels good and you resonate with the outcome. Ideally, you will relax and stay with the feeling for two to three minutes each time you run your *Genie movie-of-the-mind*.

The more realistic your *Genie* Movie feels in your quantum soup, the more energized it is. The more energized it is, the more your Universe experiences it as part of your reality. The more the Universe experiences it as part of your reality, the more the Universe will bring you what you really desire. There really is no other option.

Dealing with what you don't want

Your *Genie* Movie is barred from using words or thoughts that come from a position of "I don't want". For example, "I want to marry a man who doesn't come home drunk" is inappropriate.

If you find yourself thinking in those "don't want" terms, you will draw more of these undesirables to you because the subconscious cannot hear the word "not." Simply allow this information to lead to what you DO desire with a simple exercise. You must approach your *Genie* movie making from a visual image that is based on *desires*.

Your "don't want list"

If your mind is still filled with your "don't wants", you must first clear those from your mind. As a completely separate exercise, make a list of what you clearly do not desire. Such "don't wants" are useful to know but are not the basis of your movie script.

---

for 20 minutes a day improved by 24 percent. The group that didn't practice or visualize showed no improvement. However, the group that was instructed to visualize making perfect free throws for 20 minutes a day improved their game 23 percent! (There are many such studies. The Russians are the leaders in this field.)

In part two of your "Don't Want List" exercise, write a contrasting list that resonates on the opposite qualities you desire. What do those "don't wants" look like once you have re-framed them in the positive? Make sure you frame it as a positive *desire,* as opposed to the negative "I don't want." You will find a detailed discussion of how this is done in Chapter 9, "Tools."

Remember that you are the star—anything goes! When you are in your matrix you are in a sphere of influence that is totally controlled by you.

Mission impossible

Another problem you may encounter with your *Genie* Movie is that your visualization may arise from a world that says you cannot have what you desire. If you want to meet the perfect man, "There is a shortage of good men." may be something you have heard or thought. Your response can be "I only need one." Your movie is to avoid all of the *outside influences* that would prevent you from getting what you want. These influences may be the reality for others around you at the present, but they don't belong in your movie. Dismiss any influences that say you cannot have your outcome. This is covered extensively in Chapter 6, "Using Fear to Fuel the Genie."

Your movie making ignores any feedback that doesn't serve your outcome. This is demonstrated by the Phoenix Sequence and what you will learn about fractals (Chapter 14). You will be delighted to know that your mental process, the "Yes, but..." thought, is actually answered here!

Keep using feedback that serves you and ignoring feedback that doesn't. Negative feedback keeps a system in place; positive feedback moves it forward in unexpected leaps. This is another exquisitely orchestrated principle borrowed from Chaos Theory that, once you understand it and the larger implications, will turn you into a master manifester. Look for those leaps. Let the Universe surprise you with its achievement avalanche. The reason why this works is found in Chapter 14!

Common mistakes

Sometimes you may wish to retell your past experiences or to mull over what has happened before. It is a way to validate who you have been. It is human nature to seek validation.

However, talking about the past, especially if you are choosing to be different now, probably doesn't serve you. Since you are choosing your words carefully now, you may find it helpful to preface with, "I used to feel that in my past" or "my past life or family said, thought, etc., but now I feel…"

Your past doesn't matter

By giving yourself permission to reframe what has happened to you in the past, without re-energizing it, you have validated yourself. This releases any tension that exists around your prior circumstances. When you do not honor yourself and then create the bridge, you miss the opportunity for the quantum leap that takes you to a new and different outcome now.

Once you cross that bridge, your new outcome allows you to be different. This is important because it validates your past, ends self-recrimination and removes resistance about what could have been. In your past you did the best you could do. Now that you know more you will choose differently, and more importantly, make room in your subconscious for the NEW improved version of you who is successful, powerful, profitable, etc.

What your resist – persists

Remember, what you resist persists. Resistance will give you more of whatever you are resisting and it becomes an endless circle of creating desire, then offering resistance to what you do not want; getting more of what you don't want, and then starting over again creating desire.

You will probably get what you desire eventually, but imagine placing an order with a waiter, then calling him back and changing it, then changing it again. Pretty soon the waiter will decide to not bother sending it to the kitchen until he is sure you are serious about it. (In Chapter 7, "Your

Divinity Test," you will find helpful information on getting serious about your manifestation.)

Being judgmental about yourself or others removes energetic support from your manifestations, by offering resistance to your heart's desire. Everything that is going on in your personal sphere of influence affects the overall matrix that supports your manifestation. ("Spheres of Influence" are fully addressed in the next chapter.)

Bless each moment as perfect for who you are, or who you were. Blessing your past and making it OK sends a strong signal to the Universe to bring to you more of what pleases you. At some point you will stop talking about your past. When this occurs, you will have stopped judging it.

Sometimes you get fresh wounds to cry about. Certainly you must express your emotion, for repressed feelings are very powerful. Repressed feelings will get larger to get noticed. Think of a little child who has slammed his finger in the door.

He comes crying to you, yet there is no mark on his hand. If you ignore him, his cries for attention and sympathy grow larger. If you pay attention, the child will recognize he is acknowledged and quickly moves on to other things.

My rule for telling about a recent hurt or disappointment is three strikes and you're out. I give myself permission to tell a hurtful story three times. After that, it's out.

Second Component –Sound Stage– Lights, Camera, Action!

Write your *Genie* Movie script

Once you experience having your heart's desire, script an event that follows it. What would you naturally expect to occur after you have your heart's desire? Focus your attention on that "after-event" while bringing your feelings into the experience to reinforce it. Be sure to include that "real-time conversation" that proves you had a witness and your conversation with that person. The first time you do this, your natural response will be to start feeling real emotion as you look to the past and see you are already living your outcome. This emotion supports your emerging manifestation. This is excellent.

Remember, your movie starts at a place in time and space where you have been maintaining your desired outcome for a period of time. For example, in one class a woman wanted to live in a warmer climate. Her movie included a friend noticing her natural suntan.

Keep it real

A man in my workshop wanted to work for the Miami Dolphins. This particular workshop was being professionally recorded. When I asked him to imagine making a telephone call to someone after he had received word that the desired job was his, he said he would call his mom. To help dramatize his movie, I suggested I stand in for and role-play his mom—right in class, in front of the 100+ persons in attendance, for practice—in the conversation he would have with her.

There was a big pause, I asked what was wrong, and he said he couldn't say what he would normally say because the workshop was being recorded. I suggested he "clean up his language" and find a way to modify what he would say. So he did. "Mom, I'm working for the F—n' Dolphins." What does your mom say in response? "No F—n' way." I asked him if his mother really talked that way and he said, "Yes." Every one of our participants laughed out loud instantly when he said this! Can you imagine? Finding the joy and humor in these imagined moments are an important element of your movie. So of course his movie was perfect for him.

The movie may also contain a surprise

It's actually a very positive sign when your movie surprises you with conversations or actions that you did not script purposely. It means that you really are succeeding out there in this quantum soup of all possibilities because you are seeing something that even *your ego or conscious mind* hasn't thought of.

When you encounter surprises in your *Genie* Movie, you have used emotional resonance to create a powerful spontaneous movie that will manifest your outcome easily. (Resonance is described fully in Chapter 8, "Resistance, Resonance and Feedback.")

*It is a **VERY GOOD SIGN** if you are surprised by your Genie Movie conversation's direction.*

It means you really are in that moment in the quantum zone and your conversation is alive.

If your movie keeps changing and evolving, that is a good sign too.

It means that the quantum zone is showing you elements of the manifestation that will become part of the observed reality.

Figure 2-1

Remember, quantum mechanics asserts that from any given point all possibilities exist. In your *Genie* Movie you will use the matrix to help you imagine *that one specific point,* after you have achieved your heart's desire, from which everything is radiating in all directions. You are then situated with that projection point *behind* you in a time sequence. That point has already occurred. The mood has been set.

The Third Component – Run Your Movie

The *Genie* movie theater

Imagine your heart's desire radiating the image out in all directions like a light bulb. Because this heart's desire beams in all directions, any number of possibilities can occur. You pick one that clearly establishes the pre-existence of your heart's desire. This follow up occurrence, the *after-event*, becomes the pivotal point where the movie begins.

Some movies have a flashback. The first event in your movie is the **after-event**, the one-on-one conversation that is a direct result of having your heart's desire. Your **flashback** will be the experience of *having* your heart's desired outcome. Your first scene is always something that happens *after* you have your outcome, your flashback.

When you are in a movie theater, the projector is behind you and the movie screen is in front of you. You sit between the two. In the *Genie System*, anything you project (such as your heart's desire, the after-event, etc.) is always radiating in all directions; hence it is spherical.

On a timeline you will experience two projection points, the first one, the event (your heart's desire), is behind you. The second point is the new present moment of your after-event. Because it is spherical, when one solution doesn't work out, another one is already on its way to you. This is discussed fully in Chapter 7, "Your Divinity Test."

Your observation of it leads you to believe it occurs in a linear fashion because that is how you see it – following a timeline. However, please understand, your awareness of the event *behind* is as a **past** event. Allowing your visual image to show you what happens next creates the movie in front of you. Remember that what is in front of you, the **after-event**, is experienced as the present moment.

For example:
You desire to be with your beloved
(and you don't have one).
Your after-event is a celebration of your
anniversary (the day you met).

The flashback is of your shared joy and your
happiness together as you celebrate the
anniversary of the day you met some time ago.

Figure 2-2

Understanding the matrix

As an observed reality, all the other elements of the matrix adjust and conform to provide you with the precise outcome. You are using all the known elements of THIS matrix; linear thinking, observation and feeling. Your movie has created a linear equation by experiencing what happens after the desired outcome and creating an observed outcome. You are historically tracing a past by creating a line between an imagined *Genie* Moment present (the after-event) and past (the event). The *Genie* Moment is your heart's desire, the thing you want. You then follow a probable future from that occurrence that proves the "Genie Moment" did indeed occur.

To understand this, think about the many possible futures of a high school graduate; college, military, job, travel, etc. Looking forward, from his vantage point as a high school senior, he sees multiple versions of his future. Yet, if the heart's desire of the student is *going to college* (his *Genie* Moment), in his *Genie* Movie he looks back to that same day of planning in his senior year, from his college graduation day, knowing that the ONE thing he chose—to go to college and finish—is tangible and real.

Being present at his college graduation is the "proof" that his *Genie* Moment (his heart's desire) was successful. Of course he will need to include a conversation with someone important to him, a parent or other significant supporter to bring in the observed conversation element. This way of using your imagination, looking backwards into the past, is linear. It is linear from his point of observation of his college graduation (after-event) to his heart's desire of *going to college.* His after-event in his *Genie* Movie, the graduation, proves he accomplished this, and he is seeing it from the vantage point of having achieved it.

The matrix that we live in, typically called third dimension (3-D), is the combined energy of four different dimensions. These subsets aren't talked about much. The first one seems so obvious that it's often overlooked, that's self-awareness (1-D). The second part is the linear equation (2-D), in that it requires a distance between two points. I believe we actually use time this way, "before and after." The third part (3-D) is your "self observation." Generally this involves agreement with another human being, witnessed by a conversation that is likely, with someone who joins your observation. This is the part that "makes it real." All of quantum physics tells us that it is the *observed reality* that is real, and that the *act of observation* causes the multiple versions of the reality to collapse into just ONE reality. The fourth part (4-D) is your emotion. There is a lot of misunderstanding about what fourth dimension really is. In truth, it is the "energy" of *change* fueled by your strong feeling around an event or outcome. Think of it as emotion. It is *chi* charged with a purpose – feeling.

Introducing linear

We often refer to linear equations as formulas that allow us to substitute operators. For example, VELOSITY times TIME equals distance traveled. It is linear because you can change the two operators – of time or velocity – to produce an accurate prediction.

You use this linear equation, also known as Newton's second law, in our daily lives. For example, if you are going 60 miles per hour, and you are driving for one hour – you know that the distance traveled is 60 miles. You all use this formula anytime you drive somewhere. You don't realize that it is a classic linear formula that presumes all other factors are *equal*. Of course, in reality, other factors are not always equal. If you stop for gas or at a rest stop, or if you slow down and speed up because of traffic, any of these things will impact your final outcome. For our purposes, let's just think of the pure linear equation. None of these exceptions matter right now in understanding the concept.

Putting the pieces together

So now, how do you relate this to the manifestation exercise? You will use your awareness of yourself (1-D) looking at the past from a future outcome that is beyond your heart's desire, which produces the linear equation (2-D), and next you have a real-time (3-D) conversation with another person (observed by you in your mind) that gives you the knowledge that this event has already occurred. Observe yourself while interacting with your *Genie* Movie participant, and when you see your *Genie* Moment (the after-event) occur so clearly in your mind, your natural emotions respond with excitement and happiness (4-D) and suddenly it feels real.

This real-time conversation (imagined) is real and believable because, according to quantum science and all the experiments that confirm it, a real observed situation and a mentally observed situation are
30

indistinguishable by the brain. Your emotion confirms it. When you introduce the sacred geometry that underscores this, the Phoenix Sequence (Chapter 14), you will have your eureka moment!

Using the lighthouse

Think of the quantum soup as the way the weather looks on a really foggy day. Your movie needs a safe zone inside this "fog." You will use the "lighthouse" as that safe zone. The lighthouse will be used in other ways as well.

The lighthouse is reminiscent of a functional lighthouse that serves as a beacon in a fog to guide you to "home port." Although a traditional lighthouse would warn sailors of rocks or shoals, i.e. danger ahead, in the *Genie* Movie, the lighthouse is a *beacon from* your desired outcome, which has already occurred in the quantum field. It is a metaphor for the location where you begin your movie in your quantum zone of all possibilities. The lighthouse draws to you everything you need to manifest your heart's desire.

The lighthouse is the location of your movie theater. You need the lighthouse because you will replay your *Genie* Movie over and over in your mind's eye. It is helpful to lock into a location that is easily found in the fog. This awareness of the lighthouse in the quantum soup allows you to accept that it is real even though you don't know where or how it occurs, it just exists. The *Genie* Movie exists as the real-time experience of that after-event.

The mystery of the Phoenix Sequence enters here. It is related to the Fibonacci ratio – but much grander. I am devoting a whole section – in Chapter 14 – to explain this effect. I will show you, at this juncture, that you are now creating using the principles of linear equations. Connecting two points, your current situation and after-event, in a linear equation (using the Phoenix Sequence), compels the Universe to create your heart's desire. Letting the Universe fill in the "how" allows for the fastest, easiest solution, which you may not have any awareness of, to produce your heart's desire.

Fourth Component – Your Heart's Desire Occurs

Achieving your heart's desire

"How" becomes the responsibility of the Universe. The Phoenix formula is part of the discussion of the sacred geometry principles that undergird this reality. They will show that when you control the matrix from the original two starting points, your heart's desire must manifest. What are your two starting points? They are the *after-event* and where you are *today*. (See Chapter 14's discussion of the "Phoenix Sequence.")

Adding your emotion creates from the fourth dimension. Your emotion stabilizes your *Genie* Movie in the matrix to make the experience of your manifestation real, and thus conforms to your picture of reality. Your emotion creates resonance to signal the Universe that it is "genuine."

Utilizing multiple elements of dimensions for manifesting makes it easy for the Universe to create your outcome. Adding your emotion helps to "set" the manifestation and create resonance, which will support your manifestation. (Resonance is discussed fully in Chapter 8, "Resistance, Resonance and Feedback.")

When you reinforce your visualizations with what happens next (linear, or second dimension), your observed conversation with someone (third dimension) and with your emotions (fourth dimension) you are "resonating" elements of the adjacent dimensions to reinforce and support your manifestation. Your interactive conversation with someone anchors it into this version of third dimension as an observed occurrence and makes it easier to feel your emotion and the joy and delight of your true achievement. These components become part of the movie that you will create and run inside your lighthouse.

Funding and filling the lighthouse

The lighthouse beams out your *Genie* Movie, shining into the fog of the quantum soup. It beams out your after-event in all directions so that it can be observed and manifested.

It beams in all directions so that the best, easiest, fastest solution can present itself. Remember that there are multiple answers to your "manifestation equation" until you select one that pleases you. You don't have to accept the first one that comes along. This is also why, when one solution doesn't work out, another one is already on its way to you.

Your emotions fund the supply of power to your lighthouse with the energy of your intention. Like plant food for your garden, your emotions ensure your success. The word *funding* is used deliberately to describe the purpose of the energy as supporting and nurturing your *Genie* Movie's growth.

You are funding your heart's desire with your emotion by running your movie from within the safety of the lighthouse. In your lighthouse, you run your *Genie* Movie and you feel excitement and fulfillment. These emotions serve to fund your *Genie* Movie further, as its beams energy on the possibilities that will bring in your desired outcome—making it alive and real.

After the *Genie* Movie finishes, you will have a sense of satisfaction. This gratification creates the resonance that will draw in your desired outcome from the place of all possibilities.

Location, location, location

You run your *Genie* Movie in your lighthouse to fill the matrix that will support your desired outcome. Because this is holographic, every part of the matrix becomes your movie. It exists in the quantum soup where there are no hindering influences on this event.

In fact, there is no way that your manifestation can be withheld from you in this realm. The pinpointing of your outcome with the lighthouse beam—this act of observation—*causes* your outcome to manifest. Your feelings and emotions validate it.

The lighthouse serves as the vessel of the *Genie* Movie. It acts as a beacon directing the rest of the reality, pulling the outcome towards you effortlessly. It will help you recognize that your outcome is real, for you have seen and felt it even though you don't know *how* it will occur, or when. The lighthouse helps you stay in "neutral" so that you don't try to use logic to figure out how it will occur.

The lighthouse allows you to nurture your *Genie* Movie unencumbered by other people's observations or opinions. The more you run your movie, the more energy is fed back into the lighthouse in a positive feedback loop. As you will learn in chaos theory (Chapter 14), it is the positive feedback that creates the quantum leap into a new outcome.

There are several ways to fund your *Genie* Movie; all use emotional energy. In this chapter we have delineated the use of positive emotion. In Chapter 6, "Using Fear to Fuel the Genie," you will discover a way to use negative emotion to fund your *Genie* Movie.

Once you have created your *Genie* Movie, you don't need to go back to the "movie set" unless you decide you need to edit your movie.

Running the completed movie, embracing all that you have learned

Is there any limit to how often you can run your *Genie* Movie? You can run your *movie-of-the-mind* any time, any place. Two of the best times to run your *Genie* Movie are in the early morning before getting out of bed and at night right before falling asleep.

Summary

The matrix represents the womb, or mother. The lighthouse inside the matrix provides a safe structure for your evolving *Genie* Movie. It is a vessel or cradle to hold your *Genie* work while it grows and matures inside.

34

The matrix encompasses everything necessary to incubate your "heart's desire." It contains the *movie set* within which you "make your *Genie* Movie." It depends upon a supply of high integrity energy from the emotions and thoughts you place into it.

The matrix contains the following components:

1. Mood
2. Movie Set
3. Movie Theater
4. *Genie* Movie - Past Event – Heart's Desire

Get into a relaxed state, and allow your mind to create this visually. Pay attention to movie themes. Remember to create from your "desires" and avoid your "don't wants." It is important to validate your past to allow you to remove any resistance to it.

Begin your *Genie* Movie with your after-event, unencumbered by *how* it has occurred. The after-event becomes the *present moment* from which you will visualize this conversation about the past "heart's desire" fulfillment. The next step is to have a realistic one-on-one conversation in your mind with someone who is important to this outcome.

You must experience it as if it has *already* occurred and you are observing yourself after that experience. If you cannot imagine what happens after your heart's desire has occurred, then there is something blocking you from having it. Finding and addressing those blocks is critical to manifesting your heart's desire.

Your heart's desire and the "after-event" are anchored firmly by your *Genie* Movie's first person conversation, which enables you to utilize creation on all four dimensions. If this personal conversation surprises you, you know you've succeeded. This kind of surprise in your movie is great.

Once you have created your *Genie* Movie, it handles all the details. Your *movie-of-the-mind* holds your sacred space and mood, the set for your movie scene and the action of your conversation at the after-event. Your feelings enliven your outcome as you beam your movie through the lighthouse and broadcast it into the quantum soup of all possibilities.

Your projection point is in the center beaming out in all directions. The events are like a reverse hologram that radiates out in all directions producing your desired effect. Later in Part II, "The Principles & Proofs" section, when you understand the Phoenix Sequence and that the symmetry and order of the Universe can be harnessed to achieve your highest goals and outcomes, it will be like hitchhiking on the energy of the Universe! Everything within this holographic field is real, tangible and will conspire with your *Genie* Movie.

Run your movie as often as you like. The best times are first thing in the morning before arising and last thing before falling asleep. This repeated act of seeing yourself inside the movie causes that specific event to manifest in the real world.

By using the lighthouse image every time you run your movie, you make it possible to know that your heart's desire exists – out there – without knowing the "how's" and "why's" of its creation. In fact, it's better to leave the "how" entirely to the Universe.

Chapter 3

Boundaries and Spheres of Influence

Pasteur's nemesis

In this well-documented story,[9] a famous scientist named Pettenhoffer was outraged at Louis Pasteur's recent scientific discoveries showing that bacteria caused disease.[10] He disagreed and was so certain he was right, and Pasteur a lunatic, that he publicly swallowed a whole vial of cholera bacteria to make his point. He never got sick from it, and bragged derisively of his triumph for the rest of his life.

Pettenhoffer believed that it was the terrain of the body that determined whether disease entered! In Pettenhoffer's case, his view of the reality was based on what he believed. Yes, he scorned Pasteur, but only to elevate and hold his own belief solid.

Cell boundaries

Basic biology teaches that DNA directs the traffic and flow of biological functions, in fact, life itself. I've always thought otherwise. If it is strictly the DNA, how do we account for individuals who carry a specific genetic coding but have no symptoms? There are dozens of cases of identical twins where one has a genetic disease in full bloom, the other with no symptoms or remission.

---

[9] Szymborska, Wislawa, *Nonrequired Reading: Prose Pieces*, translated by Clare Cavanagh. In this book Wislawa, a Nobel-prize winning poet, discusses *Scientists in Anecdotes* by Waclaw Golebowiez, second edition Warsaw: Wiedza Powszechna.1968.
[10] "Pasteur's discoveries regarding germs and bacteria have since been dis-proven. http://www.healingnaturallybybee.com/articles/germ12.php

Conventional science has long held the view that this cell membrane was a "passive," semi-permeable barrier, resembling a breathable plastic wrap, whose function was simply to contain the cytoplasm.[11]

Yet the cell membranes of all cells in living organisms somehow recognize and accept beneficial chemicals, which we call nutrients. Conversely, the cell membranes also are able to recognize and reject non-beneficial foreign substances. Remember this detail, as you will use it later.

Author and researcher Dr. Bruce Lipton confirms this, saying "Studies on cloned human cells led me to the awareness that the cell's plasmalemma, commonly referred to as the cell membrane, represents the cell's 'brain.'"[12]

He continues:
> "Cell membranes, the first biological organelle[13] to appear in evolution, are the only organelles common to every living organism. Cell membranes compartmentalize the cytoplasm,[14] separating it from the vagaries of the external environment.

> "In its barrier capacity, the membrane enables the cell to maintain tight 'control' over the cytoplasmic environment, a necessity in carrying [on] biological reactions."

This frees us from genetic determinism and leads us to his conclusion that it is the cell membrane —reacting to "all perceived environmental stimuli, both physical and energetic"[15]— that is the command center of the cell, and not the DNA. His studies have led him to determine that "the 'Heart of Energy Medicine' may be found in the membrane."

---

[11] Lipton, Bruce H., "Insight into Cellular Consciousness," reprinted from *Bridges,* 2001, Vol. 12(1):5.

[12] Ibid.

[13] Ibid. An organelle is a diminutive organ system that is part of an individual cell. It contains the equivalent of digestive, excretory, respiratory, musculoskeletal, immune, reproductive and cardiovascular systems.

[14] Cytoplasm is the fluid that is the living organism at the cellular level.

[15] Lipton, Bruce H., "Insight into Cellular Consciousness," reprinted from *Bridges,* 2001, Vol. 12(1):5.

Magic of the membrane

If the brain of the cell is its membrane, and all living things have this membrane, and all membranes operate essentially the same way, and they do, you may very well have similar "energetic" membranes around your body that science has yet to perceive. It wasn't until after the invention of the electron microscope that science even had the capacity to see this cellular membrane, so perhaps our individual outer membrane is yet to be discovered.

In the *Genie System* you develop a conscious awareness of your own membranes. All of these exist around the body. I've named these membranes or boundaries "spheres of influence." Every system, be it a family, corporation, or other institution—any group that shares a common identity—has a membrane that serves as a "gatekeeper." It is this boundary that is at the core of how you create, at every level. This boundary is a basic tool of manifestation.

Boundaries

Everything has natural boundaries. If you will refer to the basic law of creation, one needs a boundary simply in order to reproduce. Why? If you have no boundary, then you have no independent existence or consciousness. You are everything.

Babies come into the world thinking they and their mothers are one, then slowly develop a sense of self and "other." This *relationship* is critical to living independently and creating.

Without boundaries there is no creation. A boundary will give you a space of similar energy or awareness to support your creation. These boundaries are called *spheres of influence.*

Spheres of influence

Each of the spheres is a reflection of the consciousness it is named after. It contains a system of beliefs that define the rules of the particular sphere. These spheres of influence function like cell membranes providing boundaries and can determine what is toxic and safe.

These spheres give us the ability to create in the reality. Collectively we have allowed these spheres to provide safety and comfort by providing rules about our three-dimensional reality, such as time and space.

It is possible to create in such a powerful way that your personal sphere of influence becomes stronger than any of the outer spheres. This allows you to step outside of the rules of the mass consciousness just as Pasteur's nemesis, Pettenhoffer did. The stronger your personal sphere the more effectively you create. Integrity is key.

As you think about Pettenhoffer, think about the times that someone has told you something about a situation that he or she believed was factual and you knew otherwise. You found yourself almost laughing at how silly, dumb, not aware, etc., the other person was. You had no need to convince them, so you just ignored or playfully scorned them and effectively maintained your personal sphere. This is one of the ways you maintain your sphere's boundary or membrane.

Five basic spheres of influence

There are five basic spheres of influence. They are: You; Family and Friends; Co-workers, Associates and Neighbors; Culture; and Mass Consciousness. Within each sphere of influence there are varying subgroups that operate in a person's reality. These spheres might not be perfectly fitted inside one another, but may cross each other randomly.

You

The innermost sphere is everything you think about. It is a system of beliefs you hold about how life works. This is really the most important sphere; so self-awareness about this is vital.

Sometimes you are your own worst enemy because it is your thoughts that hold you back. There may be several voices that you "hear" in your head. At least one is your own. These inner voices may have been labeled friendly, but they may be limiting you, too. Even if they were once true, it is important to recognize that these voices may no longer be true today.

A parent or relative's advice may have been invaluable when you were a child, yet now it does not support you. Your belief systems have grown

40

apart; they do not believe what you believe, nor do they think what you think.

It is important to clarify those inner voices to determine what is coming from the inner you, and what is coming from everywhere else! This is discussed fully in Chapter 4, "Choice."

Family and friends

This sphere is full of well-meaning individuals whose beliefs may or may not agree with your innermost thoughts. Whatever they think is their truth, and this is not necessarily what YOU think is true for you. Just because you are related to them, or work with them, or think you have things in common with them, doesn't mean that you should accept their views wholesale and put them into your system!

This group of influencers can sneak in without you realizing what has happened! If your mother always supported you, but now you have different values from her, you can selectively choose to ignore some of what she tells you without rejecting her.

How do you love them without taking on their belief systems? The key is staying true to you. As you begin to work with feedback you will begin to allow them their reality, which also allows you yours.

Co-Workers, associates and neighbors

This group of influencers generally is an arm's length away, and you can usually see them for what they are and distance yourself from them if their attempts at influencing you become overwhelming. In the next chapter, "Choice," you will find a list of phrases you can use to maintain your distance while remaining on friendly terms.

Culture

Cultural influences have a way of staying with you, especially if you were steeped in ritual or custom in your childhood. You may continue to do it "the way it has always been done," even when it no longer has meaning for you, or when the reasons for doing it that way are no longer valid.

You may have heard of the woman who was preparing a ham for dinner. The story goes that she cut it in half before putting it in the oven. When asked by her husband why she did that, she replied that her mother had always done it that way. The husband, intrigued, asked his mother-in-law who referred him to the grandmother who replied that in her day the pan wasn't big enough!

How many customs of your culture are you participating in that are counter to your beliefs, goals or desires? Have you created new customs that are in alignment with your current values? As you delve into your past, you may find that different belief systems were the motivation behind many customs that no longer apply to you.

Knowledge is power, and as you explore your own beliefs, as compared to your family's, you can see thoughts that were based on past taboos and learn from them. It's up to you to select what serves your purposes and what does not. These experiences will lead to greater discernment in how to filter feedback.

Mass consciousness

Individually and collectively we allow the reality to exist. Mass consciousness *defines* every aspect of this reality. Mass consciousness is the way the human species has agreed to operate in the world. This reality includes rules that have been defined by Einstein's theory of relativity, Newton's laws of motion, etc. Mass consciousness can include beliefs about the world as well as the known scientific laws.

Every once in a while someone like Pettenhoffer steps outside of these "laws of reality" and people are mystified as to how one was able to break free from them. In reality, his strong sense of self was the determining factor. Integrity (or lack of) contributes to the success or failure of maintaining your sphere of influence.

These spheres are the projection of our vast agreement on the reality. When individuals of like mind come together, they focus on what they have in common and devote their energy to the purpose of the group, which grows its identity.

The outlying spheres are evolving as man is evolving. Inevitably, the spheres have taken on a life of their own – due to the amount of energy and thought invested in them. When large numbers of individuals participate in a belief system, they create what is known as group consciousness. These energies are large because of the massive number of individuals who support them with their belief systems.

There are many spheres that intersect and weave through all of our own spheres. Each group consciousness dictates the rules of its sphere. I have illustrated a few of the major ones in a simplified model (Figure 3-1).

These boundaries give us the ability to create in this reality. You may find it helpful or necessary to belong to various belief systems, as they support your own energy with the massive energy of group consciousness, but it is not required that you belong to all of them.

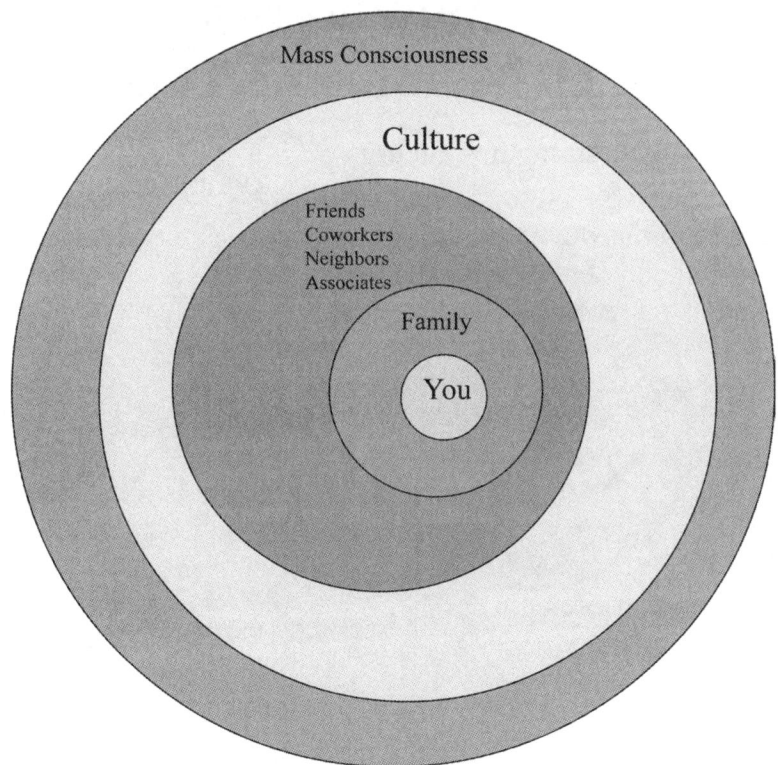

Spheres of Influence

Figure 3-1

Toxic entry

Consider, for example, how mold can get into the body. In most instances, your body will provide adequate defense to any foreign entry (Figure 3-2). Occasionally, an organism such as mold penetrates the cell membrane because it has a protein coating or some other apparently benign outer shell around it that effectively disguises it from the cell's natural alarm system. A veritable Trojan horse, if you will. Once imbedded in the cell, the mold breaks down its protective coating and proceeds to wreak havoc upon the body system.

Use this understanding of biology to help you understand that sometimes the members of an adjacent sphere will appear benevolent, but turn out not to be. In the case of toxic entry, you might allow admission because you do not recognize the individual as being toxic.

Boundaries
Cell Membrane Theory

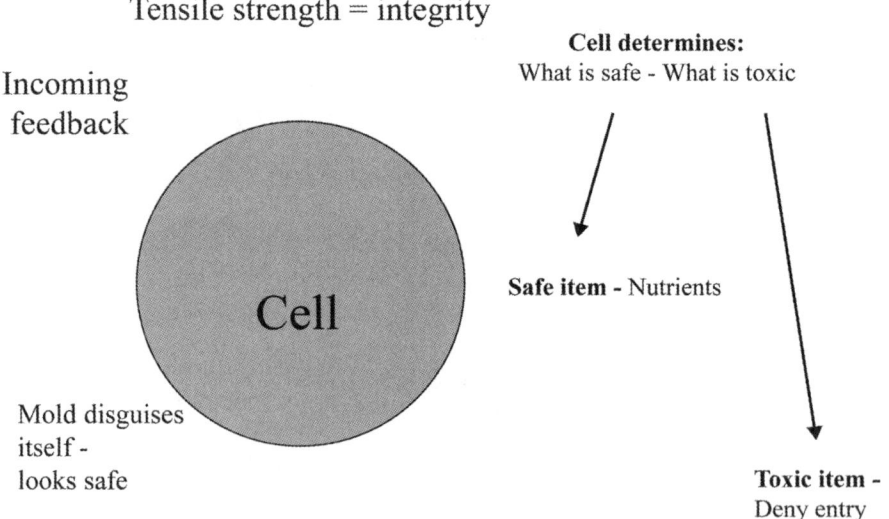

Figure 3-2

How do you maintain boundaries? Integrity! This is discussed at length in Chapter 4, "Choice." Integrity is defined as practicing the principles of ethics by making decisions based on the beliefs of equal rights for all, fairness and concern for one's fellow man. It also implies that what you hold as true for yourself will have neither preference nor prejudice towards the larger community.

Managing the spheres of influence

You must learn to discriminate carefully what you allow into your spheres of influence. As you develop your sense of self, it becomes readily apparent that you can distinguish what is "friendly" input into your sphere and how it supports your reality; and what is foreign and doesn't serve you.

There are people who are so permeable that it is as if no boundaries exist and consequently they cannot feel safe. For them, everything that happens outside the self feels like it is happening *inside*. The first step for people in this situation is to become clear about their boundaries. Deep boundary work is beyond the scope of this book. If this describes you, please seek professional assistance.

Once you have a sense of boundaries, you must learn to give yourself permission to limit the "input" (i.e. feedback) from external sources and to respect and empower yourself and your perceptions with love and acceptance. As you do this, you will slowly quit judging yourself. Then you will discover how powerful your own sphere of influence is. Finally, know that almost everyone has their boundaries (cell membrane) on "autopilot" until you decide to exercise your free will to change. You can change many things, including "the way we've always done it," all the way to "this is how everyone does it," i.e. mass consciousness. The more clearly you know and understand that you must have agreement in your thought and action, the stronger your personal sphere of influence.

Remember your experience is unique, which is why your personal sphere of influence is unique. Your version of the reality is not the only one that exists. Each person has his unique experience and thus his own version of reality, which is true for him.

All possibilities exist. You are choosing one. And, unless you are delusional, your reality is probably in general agreement with the Mass Consciousness Sphere. You are selecting, modifying and creating your own personal sphere from these spheres.

For example, two common agreements of mass consciousness include how disease works and the constraints of time. Nevertheless, you will discover even these agreements can be broken.

Other spheres

There can be large spheres besides the basic ones named. These come from large groups, but weave through many of the spheres. For instance, there is the culture of all the Hebrew nations within a Jewish person's culture. In addition, each individual will add any number of world groups that represent some element of his/her own evolution from the mass consciousness. The spheres have an expression that embodies the energy of the group consciousness they reflect.

As communication increases the world over, you will have access to beliefs and cultures worldwide. You will be able to benefit from all of the world's cultures by selecting and modifying elements of them and adding them to your own spheres.

Examining the theory of evolution, with biology self-selecting survival of the fittest, know that as mankind *spiritually* evolves and advances as a race, evolution will lead us to select the aspects that provide for our spiritual survival as well as our physical survival. Each of the spheres of influence has an energy uniquely their own and participates in this evolutionary process.

Maintaining your personal sphere

Why is the integrity of your sphere so important? For one thing, a lack of clear boundary means you are sending out "mixed messages" to the Universe. The way to maintain your own personal sphere is to stay in integrity with your thoughts, deeds and speech. You have your own value system, use it or lose it. Integrity is the sign of the strength of your own internal sphere. The more integrity you have the easier it is to manifest.

What you think is fair and honest might not be what anyone else thinks is fair and honest, although there is a general consensus and a system of laws defining right and wrong.

It can be very easy to get out of integrity with your goals and desires to "compromise" your goals and desires to conform to another's. Stepping out of integrity with your own belief system is the biggest challenge to maintaining your sphere. You won't always know when you are out of integrity, but your fear will show it to you.

Little Fear Monsters

Figure 3-3

Know that the Universe is unlimited and all possibilities exist. If you let that permeate all of your thoughts, you will find it easier to stay in integrity. There is no limit to what you can manifest.

Your spheres need the most resilient boundary possible that has fluidity and structure like fiber optic cable–strong, light, and yet flexible. Your boundary will need to stand up to the push and pull of the other spheres when the incoming feedback gives you information that doesn't agree with your stated goals and desires.

When messages arrive telling you that you have stepped out of integrity, something has to change. Either your "inner rules" must adjust so that you change your guiding beliefs, or your actions must change to reflect your beliefs. Remember that having "inner rules" that don't agree with your outer actions is the single most damaging event that can occur inside your personal sphere. Choose to stay in integrity with yourself, which will keep your boundaries strong.

Integrity indicates that your words define your actions and vice versa, so that your deeds follow decisions. It means agreements you make with others are either honored or re-negotiated, and that your internal reality aligns with your outer expression.

In simple terms, integrity means you are truthful. One of the hardest things for you to say may be "I don't know." You may be afraid to appear stupid so you may guess at an answer, say what you think the answer should be, or simply say what you think the other person wants to hear. It is never truthful to do this.

The best answers are "I don't know, but I'll look into it," or "I choose to know and I will get back to you." Or "I don't know, but based on the available information, my best guess is..." It is disrespectful to yourself and others to guess at an answer and not state that you are guessing. It is also dishonest to imply you know something when you don't.

Honesty is kind. There is an element of kindness that is most appropriate when being honest. Truthfulness that is inconsiderate or hurtful never comes from the heart. Your heart knows the difference when you are being honest or hurtful. Speak your truth from your heart. Speak the truth even if you think it makes you look bad. Speak the truth when it makes someone look better than you do. Speak the truth that holds all of us in the highest regard.

Maintaining boundaries

Maintaining your personal boundaries is the single most powerful tool you have to support your creations. Once you understand that the Universe takes you quite literally, it no longer serves you to act outside of integrity.

Some individuals have lots of integrity, others less. It is important to note that as you upgrade your "operating system," you will discover that your "new system" won't work with some of the old energy programs you used to use. You may discover that you need to change your actions. Remember that every level of integrity that you incorporate into your personal expression will increase your ability to manifest.

It may also mean that when you start to change, some of your friends may not make it into your new mode of being unless they upgrade too. Nothing can stop you. Do not waste any time on self-recrimination. Ten years from now, will it make any difference?

Weak boundaries

An example of weak boundaries could be a container filled with fresh water floating in a salty sea but has sprung a leak. The boundaries are there, but the container eventually becomes full of seawater. When you have weak boundaries, it is easier to be influenced by outside sources.

If you are committed to getting out of debt and then go on a shopping spree that is not in your budget, then you have weak boundaries, and ultimately are out of integrity with your stated goals and desires.

Boundaries and polarity

Part of the discussion of integrity includes the concept of polarity. Each of us has his or her own system of what is right and wrong. Some of us also belong to larger belief systems. For instance, if you belong to a group that believes sex before marriage is wrong and you hold that belief but act contrary to it, then you are out of integrity.

If you really do not feel OK about sex before marriage, and you are doing it anyway, you are giving out mixed signals. These mixed signals will show up in the form of fear or guilt messages, and will be more evident if you hold judgment about others' sexual behavior.

Being out of integrity usually generates fear messages. Take a look at them and see if they are coming from one of the outer spheres of influence. If they are not, and you are feeling guilty, you need to change. You need to align your inner voices with your outer actions.

Remember, rules are man-made. They are your way to create in the Universe. The game is life; you pick the rules. Pick the system of rules that pleases you and then live by it. There will always be rules, for rules are simply the ways to operate within your spheres. Without rules there is no order, no system, no boundary—no creation.

One of the most basic rules in the 3-D reality is polarity. Consider polarity to be like the positive and negative terminals of a battery. You need both of them to operate the battery. It is only in union that they can move any energy. You can use whatever rules you want, but remember to be consistent.

Benevolent king

Another way to step out of integrity is to assist someone who isn't in danger, and hasn't asked for your help. You may be so busy solving another's problems you lose track of your own. If you find yourself providing information or opinions that have not been solicited, you are crossing into someone else's sphere of influence. When you step in to solve someone else's problem, you are disrespecting their sovereignty and thus moving out of integrity with your own. You also may be motivated by something other than altruism. Whose agenda are you serving? If you have a deep concern about another's welfare and they are in danger – then of course you speak up. If it is not life threatening, consider praying for their highest and best good as an alternative to giving them your opinion.

In polite society, or in family situations, it is often easier to agree with your detractor. Let the derider think he is right—because he is in *his* world. Keep marching to the beat of your own drummer, tuning out what doesn't serve you. You may do this by saying something like, "I champion your right to hold that belief as long as it pleases you, even though I see it differently." The formula here is: a) empower with your detractor's opinion, followed by; b) state your position broadly.

Understand and recognize that these spheres of influence enable you to operate in the world. Use this knowledge to your advantage. Do not fight with the spheres. If you chose to deviate significantly from the sphere of influence of your family, or culture group, be clear on your boundaries.

The blame game

Each of the spheres of influence has a role in your world, even if it is only to help you clearly choose what you will accept and reject. This brings us to the second most significant way to step out of integrity: judging others. Judging may be pretty difficult for you to avoid. Often, when you are not busy judging others, you are judging yourself. Be careful of the blame game. It is a form of judgment. If you preface a thought with, "Well, I am not blaming him…" it is very likely that you are blaming them or yourself secretly.

Make sure that you are NOT sitting in judgment of anyone you left behind in an old sphere. They are not "wrong" and you are not "right." You are not better than they are. You are just different from them. This difference should please you. Why? Because now you have a point of contrast, and you can see clearly where you came from and what you do not want. If the difference does not please you, then you are not in integrity with yourself. You are not maintaining your sphere, you are sitting in theirs looking at yours.

The MerKaBa

If you want to learn a fast and direct way to arrive at this wonderful place of non-judgment, I suggest you consider learning the MerKaBa Classic Meditation.[16] This five minute meditation is a powerful tool that assists you to step out of judgment and stay that way.

The MerKaBa Classic uses both science and well-known meditation practices in a process that revives an ancient form of breathing. This form literally "turns on" an energy field that sits around the body.

Once activated, the MerKaBa allows one to be more connected with all of life. It enables a person's actions to come from a place of deep love and compassion.

This change in perception does not happen overnight, but with consistent practice it will happen eventually. When you no longer have judgment about yourself and others, it is much easier to manifest.

What is your belief system? Please be aware that the larger spheres have a much stronger influence on your reality than the smaller ones. The exception to this is when your personal sphere is very strongly developed and can support your being an exception to the other spheres.

The easiest way to have a strong personal sphere is to start slowly with small manifestations and work up to the bigger ones. The less mass consciousness has formed opinions about the "the way things are," the easier it is for you to create exceptions. Move in baby steps. Be consistent.

---

[16] MaureenStGermain.com, *MerKaBa Classic* meditation workshop, http://www.maureenstgermain.com/FlowerofLifeWorkshop.html.

Baby steps will take you from playing with paint like a child to being an artist who learns to work with paint and creates what he really desires. This is another benefit to having that time lag in your manifestations.

Summary

The cell's membrane is the brain-boundary which maintains tight control on what it will accept or reject. Dr. Lipton's research challenges the theory that DNA is its command center. His examination shows that it is the *cell membrane* and not the DNA that is the control center of the cell. The Cell Boundary may be the control center, but you have free will at every level of creation.

All of us have natural boundaries. These boundaries give us a homogeneous area of similar energy or awareness to support our creation. The *Genie System* has identified the major ones. These boundaries are called spheres of influence and operate like the cell membrane.

The spheres of influence are illustrated as concentric circles, but in reality are spheres. These spheres impact each other in many ways. The five basic spheres are: You; Family and Friends; Co-workers, Associates and Neighbors; Culture; and Mass Consciousness.

Within each sphere of influence there are varying subgroups that operate in a person's reality. As you look at your reality around you, be aware that there is pressure coming at you from many directions. This outer pressure is represented by the outer spheres of influence.

There will be pressure for you to conform to others' spheres and belief systems. It is helpful to belong to groups that share your belief systems, as they support your own energy with the massive energy of group consciousness. However, it is not required to belong to them.

You maintain tight control over what enters your sphere with your boundaries. Maintaining your own integrity maintains your sphere boundaries. When you are strengthening or building the boundaries of your personal sphere, one of the fastest ways you jeopardize the structure of your inner sphere's integrity is to be *out of integrity* with yourself.

It is not your place to convince anyone that they are right or wrong. Champion another's right to hold his or her beliefs–it's also good practice for learning to maintain your own.

The three ways you may inadvertently challenge the integrity of your own sphere are: 1) not being true to yourself and your own personal beliefs; 2) judging others; 3) judging yourself.

Your goal is to move from autopilot to manual within your personal sphere of influence. You are building and maintaining your own boundary so clearly, so purely, that it is both resilient and impenetrable. You want to control the feedback you *take in.* This doesn't mean controlling the feedback from outside. You may listen politely to comments you receive from others and then ignore them. Choose to keep the part that you like and ignore the rest. "Oh, you are just like your mother" becomes: "Thank you, that's the nicest thing you've ever said to me."

Just stay in a space that allows you to selectively filter. If you honor another's right to maintain his/her sphere of influence, you are also honoring your own right to do the same for yourself. The *Genie System* requires that you believe FULLY in the set of rules that govern your personal sphere of influence. They are your rules. Choose what pleases you.

The ways you can support the integrity of your system are: 1) Follow the rules of the system you belong to. If you no longer believe these rules, then consciously choose to step out of that system and find another, or make one that suits you better. You should do this by design, not by default; 2) Only offer your opinion when asked; 3) Accept others' choices, withholding judgment.

Be willing to take reasonable risks. Be willing to invest in yourself, but don't get greedy when your ship does come in. If you move in baby steps you will gain mastery faster, because you will learn from your little mistakes and not make big mistakes that will inhibit you from trying again.

You must maintain the boundaries of your personal sphere in order create your reality. Be aware that the boundary of your sphere is a living thing, just like you, just like the cell membrane. You will have "good" days and "bad" days. Remember that what you have learned from the mistakes of yesterday will help you choose wisely today. You maintain your own integrity by choice.

Chapter 4

Choice

When my youngest son was in Europe with his college choir, their return trip home was delayed at London's Heathrow Airport due to inclement weather. They were pretty tired from touring for two weeks and were headed home to the U.S. from Frankfurt through London. The first unscheduled day in London was managed fairly easily, as the hotel and dinner were provided.

The next day the young men and women returned to the airport without knowing if they would be able to fly home that day. Heathrow Airport was filled with hundreds of stranded passengers. This made some of the students very anxious and homesick.

A few of the members of his choir were lamenting that they would probably have to stay yet another day, and they didn't know *when* they would get home. Upon hearing this, my son tried to help them out of their funk by showing them what they were choosing. He stated very clearly, "Maybe *you* [the complainers] aren't going home today, but *I* am."

He was very clear in his statement, hoping they would follow his lead. He gave his fellow choir members permission to be right, yet stated clearly that he was going to have a different outcome. He told me he was concerned for them, and was trying to help them by leading them with his example!

What came as a big surprise to him and the others is that only *some* of the students flew home that day. The airline finally split the group, and his group was assigned to the flight that flew that day. The rest of the choir caught a plane home several days after the first group.

By not stepping into their version of the reality, my son maintained his integrity. At the same time, he achieved his desire of getting home *today* so magnificently. He had learned to achieve his outcome even though all available data failed to support it.

No one had thought of splitting the group until after he made his statement. Certainly it was his desire that everyone get home that day. He understood intuitively that holding his outcome firmly would affect his experience.

Hold your ground

Everyone around you can be telling you it won't work, or laughing at you for your strange ideas. All you have to do is let it glide over you, or through you. Allow yourself to hear what is being said without allowing it to penetrate your inner sphere. You can receive information, and experience someone else's reality, without accepting it for yourself. You have a choice.

One of the fastest ways someone else's sphere of influence can penetrate your innermost sphere is by your *believing* what he or she says. In show business they say you need a thick skin. In practical terms, you have to learn to hear those little zingers that get sent out, but to ignore them!

The boundary of your inner sphere should have the flexibility of a trampoline. When you jump on a trampoline, it first goes down, but then sends you up and away while it regains its flat shape.

As you look at your inner sphere, imagine it can respond like a trampoline. When a family member or friend pushes in on the sphere it dents. That is you listening to him or her. Then the integrity of your sphere bounces back and returns to its previous shape.

Separate yourself from everyone else's opinions. Take a lesson from an infamous US President. Many will remember him as a man who "didn't inhale." He claimed he knew about the dangers of marijuana and told us he selectively "filtered." So hear their bad news reports. Listen to what is happening, and learn how to "not inhale."

When I was a child, we would attempt to influence my father by telling him "But Dad, everyone's doing it." His stock answer was, "Everybody is NOT doing it, because *you* aren't. You are not doing it because you are *special*." Every single time he said it we believed him.

What others say to me: (Sometimes these are the INNER VOICES of your childhood caregiver.)	What my response to them is:
You can't do that….	My mom (or dad) taught me I could do anything, and you can too.
You think you are better than everyone else.	Everyone has his or her special gifts, including you.
Getting older is the pits.	Speak for yourself…
You can't have_____ [such as the love of your life or abundance] and be spiritual.	Watch me.
It's all about YOU…	You know we are all in this together.
You think you know everything.	And I champion your right to hold that belief as long as it pleases you.
_____, [Insert your name] this is how it is…	I can see why you might think that. I hope you will appreciate my experience. OR That is YOUR belief. I see it differently… (and I champion your right to hold that belief as long as it pleases you.)
There is a shortage of…	Maybe so, but I only require ONE.
You're so out there...	Yes, and I am so happy. Yes, you should see the view. Maybe you will join me.
(Other)	General purpose response: When in doubt, a smile is frequently a healthy and effective response in many situations. What do you care if they think you are naive or worse?

You are special, too. You are unique and can create limits on what you will accept. It's up to you to give your boundary new instructions on what gets past your gate.

If you ever find yourself saying the reason you are doing something is because everyone is doing it, please do yourself a favor and find a better reason, or give it up. Make sure you know why you are choosing and be able to say, "I choose this because it pleases me."

Be prepared

What should you do when well-meaning relatives or friends offer their opinion on what you should be doing? Be equipped with some well-rehearsed phrases. The following table should give you a jump-start on this subject.

When others make snide comments

Now that you are selectively filtering your inner sphere, you may discover that your family or friends just don't seem to be able to communicate with you. They are unable to relate to you, and start making remarks that make you feel put down or less than whole.

Your family or friends may be testing you and your new way of life. It may be that they really want to know more about what you are doing. Perhaps they are thinking about trying it for themselves.

Your unwillingness to argue with them, or make them wrong, may make the difference. Since you care about your friends and family, you naturally want to know what to say or do when these comments turn up.

When all else fails, agree with your detractor to de-escalate. For instance when you are being attacked by a statement spoken in a derogatory manner such as, "You are just like your Mother." Your response can be "Thank you, that's a huge compliment." You ignore the tone.

Envy

Earlier in this chapter you saw a list of common remarks, and responses that you can use when others discover your uniqueness. What is important here is to recognize these remarks as a form of insecurity or envy from others. They want you to be like them or they want what you have. They may be asking you about it soon enough.

Think of that famous scene in the movie *When Harry Met Sally*. Harry and Sally are having a discussion in a restaurant about their compatibility. He challenges what she says, and to prove her point Sally noisily goes into a faked orgasm, and the camera flashes to an elderly woman who says, "I'll have what she is having."

It is one of my favorite lines and I use it often to tell the Universe that I am in alignment with something that I don't necessarily understand, but which looks so good to me that I desire it, too. Go ahead and ask, "I'll have what she is having." The choice is yours.

At first, envy from another feels uncomfortable. After all, you love your friends, and you want them to be happy. If the Universe is a restaurant and you can order what your friends have, then why can't they order what you have? The Universe always has plenty of tonight's special.

Your friends can choose to have what you have. But how do you tell them that? You don't. You keep your silence. You wait for them to ask you. Hold your counsel until they decide they want to know by directly asking you.

If you experience envy from anyone close to you, find out if you are offering any resistance. You may be surprised to discover you are "feeding" his or her envy! You may be surprised at his or her behavior. That is OK. Just make sure you aren't judging him or her. The best thing to do is to continue to spend time with your close friend and support your friendship as you have always done for one another, and to do nothing about the envy. Their envy is not in your jurisdiction.

There is no point in resisting or being upset about their behavior, as that will cause more of the same. What do you care if no one else in the restaurant orders what you ordered? You still can enjoy your meal. So when your friends and family behave in an unkind or envious manner, remember that they may be wishing to have what you have.

Initially, some of your friends and family may not believe that your *Genie* manifestation work is possible. If they did, they would not need to make derogatory remarks to you in the first place.

It is also possible that when you stop giving others grief for their envy the whole dynamic will evaporate. If they can see you are perfectly happy right where you are, they may lose interest in finding ways to make you happy their way.

Self-Talk

Voices will pop up showing you "objections" as to why you cannot do something, or why something won't work. I call this "self-talk" and have listed a few below.

You'll notice my emphasis on "choose" over "want." That is because a "want" is a state of becoming compared to "choose" which is a present state. Avoid using "not" in a statement—your subconscious will only see the verb. Adding "not" before it has no impact. So here's how the subconscious interprets the following statements:

> *I will not overeat.*
> *Subconscious Interpretation: I will overeat.*
> **Instead: I will eat perfectly to maintain my ideal weight.**
>
> *I will not get angry.*
> *Subconscious Interpretation: I will get angry.*
> **Instead: I will remain calm regardless of my situation and surroundings.**

Next you need to address the inner voices of your parents, grandparents, caregivers, etc. Sometimes you don't realize their voices, and their thoughts, are being expressed. If you pay attention, you will discover some of your thoughts are borrowed.

Maybe your parents, or some other family members, were trying to give you good skills for adulthood, such as the delay of gratification. Now that you are an adult, you do not need their reminders from days past. You can remove them now. Just like you remove braces once your teeth have straightened, the old constraints have served you well and now can be discarded.

New language for self-talk

Old language	New Language
It has always been like this…	Going forward I am finding…
I am on a diet…	I am eating wisely…
I need to lose…	I am moving to my ideal weight.
I get lost all the time.	I find my way easily.
I don't have enough time.	I use my time wisely. I have an abundance of time. I find there is enough time for all that is important to me.
I promise not to get angry.	I choose to be in a loving space.
If only I were… Taller Smarter Prettier Skinnier	I have accepted who I am and I love myself unconditionally. I am now becoming the person I've always wanted to be and I am better than I thought. I am attractive to the people who matter. I see myself at my ideal weight.
Sometimes I feel small and disregarded.	Others honor me for what I bring to the table and there is always someone who will appreciate what I have to offer.
I never…	I easily… I would like to learn…
Life is always a struggle.	Life flows easily. I am in the flow. There's an angel on my shoulder.

You may think you don't have negative self-talk, but as you look at these statements in the table they may sound familiar. You may discover you are doing these things inadvertently. This self-talk is real and it can be corrected.

Make a list of your common self-talk. After you have made your list, make a "new language" list like the one below. Learn to hear these alternate statements in your head.

Re-write these statements if necessary to fit your personal experiences.

Becoming aware of your own self-talk is very empowering. Once you are aware of it, make sure you do the writing exercise so you can get the thoughts out of your mind and in front of your eyes.

It is only then that you can observe their damaging effect on your reality. Once you write them, wait a few days for the re-writes to show up. Play with this exercise. Ask your friends for good replacements of the statements you can't seem to get rid of. You will be amazed at the great suggestions that you will hear. Then record the rewrites into a tape player and play them back every morning for a few weeks so that you can get used to hearing the replacement phrases and apply them to your day.

Another common pitfall of your inner voices or self-talk takes the form of what you *don't want*. Emphasis on what you don't want pulls more of the same to you. Choose what you "desire" versus what you "don't want." For example, avoid saying "I don't want a spouse like the last one," instead say, "I want someone who treats me well." Or simply, "I desire happiness."

Self-sabotage basics

You may be far more afraid of success than failure. Perhaps you may truly desire success but fear what will happen if you are successful. Why? You crave what is familiar, even if what you have created before no longer pleases you. The familiar is safe because it is known. Everything else is frightening, which is why you crave what you already know.

When you are not in integrity, the Universe uses the ambiguity in your thoughts to create ambiguity in your world. Once you understand that the Universe takes you quite literally, and provides you with exactly what you have sent out, you no longer need to act outside of integrity.

One of the ways your manifestation may elude you is through self-sabotage. You might even catch yourself in the act. When you ask yourself, "Why did I sabotage buying a house?" you may discover that you don't trust the Universe enough to believe that you will be able to pay the mortgage, utilities, and other expenses of home ownership. Self-sabotage can be a good thing. It can tell you that you aren't ready to take on this big manifestation.

You could manifest the house of your dreams and then not be able to afford maintaining it! Losing it that way would be far more devastating than if you didn't realize your dream in the first place. By moving slower, you gain mastery and confidence in yourself and the Universe.

Why do we sabotage?

Have you ever rented a moving truck? Rental trucks from the national chains will not go above a certain speed limit. No matter how far you press on the gas pedal it will not go any faster. The reason is a piece of equipment called a governor. Rental moving trucks are designed for individuals who have little or no experience driving trucks. Why?

Truck driving is an art. If you have never driven a truck, you might think there is nothing to it. But it takes training and experience to learn how to handle heavy loads in all kinds of driving conditions. Speed and unfamiliarity breed accidents. The governor on your rental truck keeps you and the truck safe by limiting your speed.

There are governors on all kinds of equipment to cap the speed to prevent them from breaking or running out of control and causing damage. Any excess energy over and above the speed cap is thrown away or given an escape valve. The governor keeps the machinery safe.

How does that relate to your manifestation? You are in a place of inexperience in your *Genie* work. You are in a zone where you are learning how to manifest. If you go too fast you could lose control and fail. You may find yourself using self-sabotage to slow yourself down (to stop the progress you don't feel ready for) so you don't self-destruct.

You may have heard stories about the millionaire lottery winners who end up bankrupt. The percentage of lottery winners this happens to is very high. They needed something to slow them down before they self-destructed. Self-sabotage is a form of governor, in that it steps in to

63

prevent a disaster. Very likely your sabotage is preventing you from making a large mistake. Remember to bless the sabotage that you have created, and see it as beneficial, because it means you need to gain more mastery. Look for what you can learn, use your tools and then start again.

A woman in consultation with me wanted a Jeep Cherokee. A friend of hers told her that a Jeep Cherokee doesn't have legroom, and that since she is tall she wouldn't be happy with it long-term. If you get a message like this from someone about something you have already picked out in your mind's eye, you are being given a signal from the Universe.

The *Genie* method of manifestation does not rely on you to visualize exactly how something will look physically. The purpose of the image is to experience the feeling of driving that perfect car. How do you *feel* as you drive it?

A friend who tells you the shortcomings of your perfect car may be a messenger from the Universe, and there may be a possibility that the car of your dreams won't make you happy. Wouldn't you rather have that message before you purchase it, so you can clean up your visualization? This is information that you should take as a blessing. It also means you might want to go out and test-drive your dream car to see if those concerns are valid for you.

There is a fine line between a friend who is sabotaging you and one who is a messenger from the Universe. The way to know the difference is to look at the general messages that you get from that friend. Do they generally support what you desire and what will be good for you? If your friend is consistently supportive and loving, and champions your highest desires, then he or she is very likely to be the messenger of the moment.

Subconscious resistance

Is it hard for you to imagine what it is like to achieve your heart's desire? Do you feel "funny" or embarrassed about your desire? If you feel self-conscious about it, maybe you are judging people who have what you'd like to have.

For example, have you ever walked by a beautiful car, and gazed at it longingly? If you were with someone they might say, "Wouldn't it be nice to own that?" Yet something you admire or find luxurious may elude you.

Sometimes you may not know why you cannot visualize the specific thing that you desire yet you may have no trouble seeing most other things within your mind's eye.

Some kinds of sabotage (or unconscious resistance) are from deep inside of you. It is this kind of feedback that serves you because it helps you discern why you are holding yourself back. It could be that you don't feel you deserve it.

Perhaps you put yourself in a different category from those who have what you do not have. This could be an unconscious feeling that prevents you from bringing it into your experience. Discovering and understanding the resistance will help you address it.

Limitations

Who is your source? The Universe. What are the limitations? None, except for the ones you place on yourself. Your only limitation is your ability to believe and hold to your outcome. Think of the famous line from the movie *Field of Dreams:* "If you build it, they will come."

Being really clear about what you desire doesn't mean you have defined it perfectly. It means that you have clearly *felt* what it feels like to have ownership and to use it. This means you "go to your bottom line" as they say in the business world.

The bottom line is the final outcome, taking into consideration all the factors. Your goal is to savor the feeling of it, without being so precise that you limit the good that comes to you.

Focus on how awesome it feels to take your car to your place of work, drive the kids to soccer games, take your dogs for a ride, or easily haul groceries. Then it won't matter what kind of SUV it is.

Belief systems

In one workshop, a woman was easily able to visualize other things but was unable to visualize a new car that she desired. When asked what color it was, she could not see it in her mind.

It was very apparent she had some sort of mental block preventing her from experiencing her new car. This block wasn't about deserving it, yet it had to do with an issue that would prohibit her from getting it.

In her case it was a simple matter to discover. Asked, "If you had a new car, what would happen that you don't want to experience? "Car payments," was the immediate response.

Most people in the United States finance their cars. In questioning the familiar, she was asked, "Would it be possible to have a car without having car payments?" "Yes." "What kind of a car has no car payments?" "One that is paid for," was the easy reply.

Some things are so obvious. Yet you can miss the obvious because you are stuck in a belief system based on group consciousness such as how most cars are purchased.

In her case, the car she currently owned worked well and looked great, but it was an older car and was paid for. She liked the idea of having something newer. Releasing that block, and visualizing a car that was paid for, made it possible for her to see it in her mind's eye. Knowing what her car would look like enabled her to manifest her highest version of her car.

You can have your heart's desire. It is your choice. Choice is a way to experience the reality that enables you to claim your power.

Find the highest expression

Your job is to go to the highest and most evolved version of what it is you desire. Your manifestation isn't about a specific car, but about *transportation*. The highest and most evolved version of your car might be a Lexus SUV.

How will you feel when you're behind the wheel of the car that does everything you have on your list? It can hold your dogs, your equipment, and will easily be able to take you to the places you need to go. As you see yourself driving it, you feel pleasure about how easily this vehicle fulfills its function.

Identify and then feel the qualities you will experience once your heart's desire is achieved. Then express it to the Universe, "Maybe it doesn't have to be a Lexus to do all of these things." You have just opened yourself up to receive the most benevolent outcome that the Universe can provide for you. It also means that you will probably manifest transportation quicker than requesting a specific make and model of transportation.

What does the highest version look like?

When you are looking for money for college, create a *Genie* Movie that represents getting that diploma. If you desire to be happily married then see yourself celebrating your fifth, tenth or higher anniversary. If you desire a job that will please you – where they like you as much as you like them—then see them promoting you or giving you a bonus.

The following is a fictitious story about a Mom who is planning to get her son a car for his high school graduation. She doesn't have a lot of money, so she is planning on getting him a used car.

In the background is the fact that she knows she has some inheritance money coming. Then the will clears probate court earlier than anticipated and she finds that she has a lot more money than she thought. She has plenty to put away for her own retirement and to do something special for her son.

Her new plan is to provide the most fabulous car that she can imagine for him. She decides she wants to surprise him. Meanwhile, he has been looking at used cars and finds a honey of a used car. He tells his mom he found his dream car.

Originally, they thought they could get a used car for $3,000. His "dream car" is $6,000. He thinks he is outside of the budget by $3,000. She has been thinking about buying a new car, with all the options, in the price range of $30,000. She doesn't say anything. After all, she doesn't want to give away her surprise.

Since he doesn't know about his mom's surprise, he believes he hasn't convinced her—so he keeps telling her how great this car is. Pretty soon, she starts thinking that maybe she shouldn't be spending so much of her inheritance money on him this way.

Since she is convinced he will be happy with this used car, why buy any other? So she gives him what he says he really wants —the used car— when he could have had a brand new one. The Universe can do this too. You must learn to allow the Universe to bring you your highest and most benevolent outcome.

Have you ever picked up the tab for someone's meal and he or she joked, "If I'd known you were buying I would have ordered something more expensive?"

If you are sabotaging yourself, recognize that you've blown your "safety valve." This is to keep you from making too big a mistake. Find out what is going on, examine your actions and thoughts and learn from them. Go slowly, be patient and recognize your slow moving manifestations give you mastery.

Remember, the Universe conspires to give you more of what you are putting your attention on. You can "order" anything you want from the menu of the Universe, so focus on the highest expression of your heart's desire. Just remember that some things take longer to prepare and serve than others.

Summary

Every day, in every moment, you have a choice about the thoughts you think. Choice will come up over and over, a hundred times a day. Even when you default, or "go along with the crowd," you are exercising your choice.

Your choices can lead by example. Setting an example is as close as you should get to telling someone else what he or she should do.

Be prepared to be pleasant but firm when well-meaning family and friends question you. If you experience envy from others, be sure you are not offering any resistance or judgment. Continue to love this person and ignore the envy.

Monitor your self-talk with a journal and replace your comments with empowering thoughts.

When you get a message that your dream won't make you happy, pay attention. The Universe is showing you that maybe your desire won't suit you the way you had hoped, or that you inadvertently may be sending conflicting messages to the Universe.

Remember, the Universe conspires to give you more of what you are putting your attention on. You can "order" anything you want from the menu of the Universe, so focus on the highest expression of your heart's desire. Just remember that some things take longer to prepare and serve than others.

You make decisions based upon your needs and desires. This is an ever evolving dynamic that you create as you move through life experiences. Choose to find the joy where you are, and the Universe will give you MORE joy. This will start a chain reaction that will cause more and more joy to find *you*.

Chapter 5

Tips for Making Movies

Ten or more years ago, when I first started writing the material that later became this book, I began to wonder what to call this material on manifesting. I began to say to myself, "It would be a lot easier to write a book if I knew the name of this body of knowledge that I am working on."

The next time I ran my movie, I found myself having a conversation with someone about this manifestation work. In this "movie-of the-mind" I saw myself in the future looking back at what had occurred after my book had been written. I heard myself calling it by name. When I finished my mental movie I was so excited! Now I knew what to name it!!!

I went into that quantum zone of possibilities after my book had been written and published and the one possibility that gave me my heart's desire had a name. In the course of the conversation that I was both observing and participating in, I heard myself say, "Genie in the Bottle." Several years later I read in one of Jack Canfield's books, "The Success Principles," where he described a similar process; going into meditation, looking for that "perfect name" to call the material that later became known as the "Chicken Soup" series, but began as "Chicken Soup for the Soul."

I now tell people that I journeyed to the future to find out what I named this book. It could also be that I journeyed to the quantum zone to get the most compelling name for this body of knowledge that would create my desired outcome.

Indeed, one of the leading physicists in the UK, David Deutch tells us, "The universe we can affect we call the future. Those [universes] that affect us, we call the past."[17]

---

[17] Folger, Tim, "Physics' Best Kept Secret," *Discover Magazine,* vol. 22, no. 9, September, 2001.

In this chapter you will learn tips on making your *movie-of-the-mind* to create the future you desire. Don't worry about *how* this will occur. You are the navigator and the decision-maker of the desired outcome. The Universe will get you where you want to go. How do I know this for sure? Well, would you tell a taxi driver that picks you up at LaGuardia airport in New York City which of the 7 bridges or tunnels to take? Somehow, he or she KNOWS. That's the deal with the Universe. It will automatically find the most direct route to your manifestation if you will simply define the destination.

Finally you are ready to make your movie and fund your outcome with its "after-event." When your movie is ready, view it from the movie theater inside your lighthouse.

Creating from favorable states

In the movie business there are location scouts. These scouts look for environments that look like the image the movie director or screenwriter has in mind. Scouts have chosen the deserts of the southwest to stand in for the Sahara Desert and alien-looking landscapes to represent Mars. When your own environment won't work, be your own location scout and find a better one.

If you have trouble imagining your desired outcome, use an experience from your past. Select the environment that makes it easy for you to create your movie, by letting your imagination take you to a location that creates for you the same feeling as your desired outcome. Draw on a previously successful outcome and base your new outcome on it.

Create from favorable states of mind

A woman in one of my workshops wanted to have a lovely party for her son's Bar Mitzvah. Barbara struggled with her feelings of inadequacy and lack of acceptance in her synagogue. We invited her to draw from her memory the feelings of having successfully hosted a party in her past.

Barbara struggled to find something and I kept moving her back in time until she could say, "Yes, that was a great party." It turned out to be her wedding, which was a very satisfying affair.

You may go as far back in time, as necessary, until you find a feeling that resembles the one you would like to have! This is what creating from a "favorable state" is all about.

Barbara started with everything about her wedding. All the details worked perfectly. The day was wonderful. Then she moved her awareness to the following day, and imagined the day *after* her wedding, with all the requisite happy memories, reviewing the prior day's events, the good time had by all, the careful planning that led to a successful party, and so on. Barbara reviewed it in her mind's eye, so that it filled her with happy emotion all over again.

Once the joyful feelings were strongly anchored in her mind and body, she allowed herself to switch her awareness to the day after the Bar Mitzvah she was planning. She made sure those feelings were strongly anchored in her mind and heart before she mentally replaced the day after the Bar Mitzvah for the day after the wedding.

Ride someone else's rainbow

If your best friend lands the perfect job and you are thrilled for him or her, feel your joy—then jump into your movie and keep it going for you!

Superheroes

Sometimes the role you need to play is so large and overwhelming you cannot imagine how you could possibly do it. Just call in the superheroes. Let Superman/woman or James Bond do what seems impossible. Let the superhero save the day, then imagine it again, with *you* in the superhero's costume, achieving the "impossible." Remember, your job is not to see how it occurs, but to envision the completed event!

When there is no way for you to figure out how your movie should look, take the superhero approach. If you have seen some movie hero or heroine handle this kind of situation, then let him or her handle yours. Then see yourself being that hero. Simply trade places once the movie is firmly imagined in your mind. *Suspend your disbelief* and allow yourself to be the star of this movie.

This is especially helpful if you are in circumstances where you feel like you are faced with "mission impossible." Since this is all occurring in your imagination, why not go where others have not gone?

A real superhero

In 1954, the conventional wisdom was that an athlete could not run a mile in less than four minutes because the human heart would burst from overexertion. Roger Bannister, a medical student intern and amateur runner who had little time to train, determined he would break this barrier. He did not believe conventional wisdom. It was his "mission impossible," as we would say today.

Bannister broke the four-minute mile barrier on May 6, 1954. While there were better trained athletes in superior condition elsewhere in the world, Bannister was the visionary to break the record. These other athletes had believed it was impossible—until they saw Bannister's feat. Then they *knew* it could be done.

Within a month, the Australian runner John Landy had broken Bannister's record. At that summer's British Empire Games, in a race billed as "The Mile of the Century," both runners beat the four minute time, with Bannister coming in first. This demonstrated that the four-minute mile was as much a psychological as physical barrier.

Video-game stars

You can be the star of a video game. I remember when one of my sons played the Mario Brothers video game. Mario always looked like he was going to step right off a cliff. Yet when my son played Mario Brothers, there was always a piece of dry land coming out of nowhere just as Mario stepped off the cliff. (I later learned from my son that this happens only when you are good at the game, but that doesn't matter, because the only version I ever saw was the successful one.)

At one point in my life, I was extremely worried because I was about to lose my day job. My employer was being taken over by a larger company that didn't need our management team. All the managers knew we were slated to get pink slips.

Despite this foreknowledge, I could not imagine what could possibly save me from the potential cliff that I surely was headed for. I had been looking for a replacement job for quite a few months without success. I was so afraid that I could not imagine how I would continue to support my family with my current debt load and no savings or resources.

In the movie that I made for myself, I imagined that I was Mario, and that it didn't matter **what** dry land came up, so long as I didn't fall off the cliff. Sure enough, I was let go and my seminar business took a big leap that summer. For the four months that I didn't have a "regular" job, I was able to generate enough seminar income to keep me going.

Focus on *what*, not how

Your job is not to decide how your heart's desire will occur or with whom. Your job is to decide what and where. Once you have determined the destination of your manifestation, you can imagine what that feels like.

The Universe automatically fills in the outline you have created. The Universe determines how it will happen and what needs to happen to fulfill your heart's desire. Trust the Universe to fulfill your desire perfectly.

Imagine traveling somewhere by car. You can be the driver, or you can have a chauffeur. If you allow the Universe to do the driving for you, you will discover how enjoyable the ride can be, and how perfectly the outcome is managed for you.

If you wish, you can request the driver take a certain route, just like you might ask a cab driver in New York to use the Lincoln Tunnel, rather than the George Washington Bridge, to get you to New Jersey. Remember, the less concerned you are about *how* you achieve your heart's desire, the more easily you will manifest it. Non-negotiables will slow your *Genie* manifestation work.

Non-negotiables

In one of my *Genie* workshops, there was a woman who was married. Her husband had a lot of concern about how she lived her life. He was very troubled about her choices, and felt she was destined for hell and damnation. He felt her behavior (for example, she didn't go to church) was a reflection on him and it bothered him a lot that she led her life differently from him.

They were both retired, and had grown children, and wanted to preserve their marriage. They both had their reasons for staying together, yet she was looking to experience her life differently from what was currently going on in her marriage. I worked with her goals and desires. We treated the marriage as non-negotiable. We created the movie that gave her an outcome that she wanted with her husband in the picture.

Of course we imagined that she found him more accepting, and that her changing would allow him to change and evolve as well. At the end of the workshop she said, "You are the first person I have ever worked with on changing my life who didn't tell me to leave him." You can have as many non-negotiable items as you wish, but these limitations will lengthen the manifestation time.

The fewer non-negotiables you have, the faster your manifestation. Everyone has non-negotiables. If you want to meet your beloved and you are heterosexual, you want your beloved to turn up as the opposite sex. This may seem like an obvious non-negotiable. But it is a non-negotiable. If you desire a new job that is within driving distance of home your non-negotiable is its *location*.

You can choose whatever pleases you. It is your birthright. Remember to keep your non-negotiable items to a minimum. Look closely at the non-negotiables in your movie to be certain they are what you truly desire. Treat them like difficult movie stars that have to have a certain kind of food delivered, or who will only work under certain kinds of conditions. You are the star. Let the Universe take care of everything else.

What if it doesn't work out?

If you meet your dream partner and it doesn't work out with that particular person, *stay in your gratitude energy*. You are that much closer to achieving your manifestation. If you tell the Universe it has to be *"Henry"*— and *"Henry"* is no longer willing— it will never happen.

Feel your pain briefly, and then put your attention right into all the wonderful things you learned and experienced through "Henry" without requiring him to *be* the dream partner. If you seed the Universe with your grief by being unhappy about this for days or weeks or months, you jeopardize your matrix—because you are now creating feedback that says you cannot have your heart's desire.

Staying in your gratitude for all that you did gain will enable you to keep sending "love and gratitude" to the Universe, and the Universe will fill your order for that. Surprisingly, some of the people who have chosen to experience their loss in this way have discovered that "Henry" has come back into the picture. If he doesn't return, a replacement is close behind him, and will be so wonderful as to make it easy for you to forget "Henry." Stay in gratitude.

Believability

In *Genie* Movie making there are lots of tricks of the trade, just like in real movie making. Because your movies are movies-of-the-mind, you have no constraints of budget. You do have constraints as to believability.

When you use an already existing scenario, such as "Mario Brothers," you have already seen it on the video game, so its believability comes from there. If you cannot imagine it, and cannot find some analogy to make it viewable, you will not be able to manifest it. This is really the subject of an entire book, but bears mentioning here.

The light at the end of the tunnel

While working on this book, I was walking back to the little apartment that sits at the end of the property where I was staying. There were no lights to guide my way. I found myself instinctively turning off my flashlight as I approached the apartment. I had traversed this path many times in the past week, and felt that I knew my way very well. It was a cloudy night, and there was not a speck of light from the full moon, which I had hoped to see.

Without the light from the flashlight, suddenly it was much darker than I expected it to be. In my workshops, I talk about the personal distance that one naturally is aware of in a darkened space. I thought about my own distance awareness.

I tried to imagine how far into the dark I could see. As my eyes adjusted, I became aware of a little speck of light coming from inside the apartment, over thirty feet away, through the space between the door and floor.

My mind immediately flashed to the concept of the lighthouse that lights the way in the fog or dark. In the *Genie* work, one of the functions of the lighthouse is as a movie theater. The lighthouse runs the movie of our life after the desired outcome has been achieved. This movie beams out into the quantum soup. Those beams create connections in the quantum zone that cause the reality to shift and conform to create your heart's desire.

That little bit of light between the door and floor enabled me to keep my pace, and move easily to the entrance of the apartment, which was ten times beyond my normal comfort zone.

When you run your movie and give yourself permission to be in emotional bliss, you will feel your "heart's desire" with such strong emotion that you will already have your outcome. Your lighthouse beams out that event, and even if it is only a faint glimmer, it will serve to guide you easily into the situations and steps that need to occur to manifest your heart's desire.

Dare to dream big

In 2003, a man by the name of Sheeraz Hasan came to America without money or connections, yet he became the film industry's ambassador to South Asia – all within four months of arriving. How did it happen? He was in the right place at the right time. Without knowing, he was practicing many of the *Genie* principles.

A practicing Muslim, he was doing his daily prayers at the foot of the "Hollywood" sign, and met an influential filmmaker, Michael Levy. Levy was so impressed with him that he opened the doors for Hasan. Within six weeks, equipped with his terrific idea and his passion, Hasan had a contract to produce a show that ultimately aired throughout India.

Making movies you will star in

✓ *Don't worry about how.*
✓ *You are the navigator. You are the decision-maker. The Universe will get you where you want to go. (You can be the driver, but if you are the passenger in a limousine, you can focus your thoughts on other things.)*
✓ *Create or construct the atmosphere that makes it easy to feel strong emotion.*
✓ *Make your movie & fund your outcome and its "after-event".*
✓ *Run your movie in the lighthouse.*

Figure 5-1

Movie failures

Dream big, but be sure to incorporate your successes as they occur. If you create some really large manifestation, and have not managed to find a way to adjust and integrate it into your life, you will have a bigger chance for failure. This big chance for failure has to do with many factors, including some hidden factors of self-worth and other conditioning that you may not be aware of. (See Chapter 8, "Resistance, Resonance and Feedback" for more on this subject.

You are the center of your Universe.

Around you are an infinite number of possible futures coming from the quantum zone of multiple realities.

Figure 5-2

Three lessons from the stock market:
Greed, Risk Management and Venture Capital

Greed

One time when I was sitting in one of the airport waiting rooms, I ended up being part of a conversation between two men who were sitting on either side of me. The first man was taking about a certain stock that had done very well.

The second man said he had done well with it too, but had hung onto it too long, and lost all of his gains. He wanted to know how the first man had known when to sell. The first man said sincerely, "I decided the amount I wanted to sell the stock for when I bought it. When it moved to that price, I sold." Amazing. The second man nodded in agreement stating, "I could see how fast it was growing and got greedy."

Decide in your movie what will please you and feel grateful for it. Remember to honor your agreements. Don't let greed or fear alter them. Fear and greed can compromise your integrity. Make course corrections to stay in integrity.

You are tapping into an endless supply and there is no need to take more than what you need. If you get greedy you are telling the Universe you think there isn't enough.

It may sound silly, but take this part very seriously. Don't pick up more soap and shampoo in hotels than you can use. Take only what you can eat at the buffet. Honor what is provided for you, and act like there is an infinite supply. You can always go back for more.

Risk Management

I was sitting next to an investment fund manager on one of my many flights and we began to talk about my book. I told him about risk management and he told me that so many people are risk averse. We talked about how believing in yourself could be a risk.

Would you invest in you? If not, then change your inner sphere. If you won't invest in you, look at your belief system. Why don't you believe in you? Find out why you would not invest in you, and then do something about it.

Many people know that H. Ross Perot made his millions in the stock market. What is not generally known is that he made his money from a small section of his portfolio that was in "high risk" stocks. The way he managed his portfolio was to place ten percent of it in high-risk markets. He figured he could afford to lose this ten-percent at any time, and that if any part of his high-risk portion of his portfolio yielded; the payoff would be huge. He was right.

Think of managing your risk. Keep your agreements and don't get greedy. When you are out there in that quantum zone holding out for what you really want, be clear about it. When your heart's desire does appear, make sure you are grateful for it and accept it. Limit your risk to the ten-percent you can live with losing.

Venture Capital

One of the benchmarks all investors look for in funding a business venture is whether the entrepreneur has invested any of his own funds.

If you are hoping to obtain seed capital for your business venture, you will be evaluated by your willingness to invest in yourself.

If you aren't willing to take a risk on you, why would anyone else? How can the Universe invest in *you* if *you* won't? What are you willing to invest to achieve a dream?

Did you know that Conrad Hilton, the founder of the first successful hotel chain in America, went bankrupt five or six times before he hit upon the idea that would make him and his heir's millionaires?

Infuse your movie with your passion! Passion leads to breakthroughs. Learn to develop that passion so you can call it up at will. This will take practice; one way to do this is to become aware whenever you are passionate about something and then pay attention to how this feels in your body.

For example, you might be passionate about music. If you were asked, "Tell me the name of your favorite song," could you? How can you request your favorite song if you cannot name it? Pay attention to what you are passionate about, so that you can bring the fire of your feelings into your movie.

Going 45 in a 60 mph zone or baby steps

Move in baby steps. This admonition is very important. If you try to carry too much of anything you will drop all of it. What good will that do you? When you are working on your dream list, keep the big items separate from each other in your movies.

Conduct your *Genie* work on each manifestation separately. Allow yourself the room to experience little successes so that you are able to build confidence with each step along the way.

Early in my years as a single mom with more obligations than income, I was getting lots of those overdraft forms in the mail from my bank telling me that I had overdrawn my checking account.

To manifest the solution of overdrawn checks I did not instantly think of having more money. At that time, I knew too well what my status was. My monthly obligations exceeded my income. It was very clear that I did not have enough money to pay all of the household expenses, much less pay a big tuition bill of $5,000 a year.

Instead, I imagined my delight in going through the mail and not finding a single envelope with a bank overdraft notice in it. After I had experienced that for a period of time I moved to a bigger picture.

Next I imagined what it would be like to have an extra $50. I worked with what that would feel like. Then I increased it to $100 to see what that would feel like.

Each step of the way I was able to maintain that pleasurable feeling of having enough money in my account to pay bills and grow the balance in my checking account. Then I asked myself if I could imagine what it would be like to have an extra $500 in my checking account, then $1,000 then $5,000 then $10,000 and so on.

At each increment I allowed myself time to adjust and see what it would feel like. This took place over the course of several years. At each increment, I made sure I could accept the visual image. If my movie had been too "out there" it would have been impossible for me to maintain it.

Another reason to move in baby steps is to learn to be mindful. If you could manifest everything you could think of, you could accidentally manifest things you did not desire. You would be overwhelmed by all the stuff that would clutter up your world and confuse you. This is why there is a time lag in manifestation. The Universe gives you time to be clear that you really desire what you are asking for.

Baby steps let you take advantage of the learning curve. Sixteen-year-olds with learner's permits aren't likely to be given a brand-new car with which to practice driving. In some states, they won't allow an inexperienced driver with a new driver's license to oversee someone who is learning to drive. The same is true for you. You don't want to start out manifesting something significant without first gaining some mastery in the system.

By moving in baby steps, the checks and balances of the process go into place as you learn to manifest. One of the reasons you manifest in steps is that each experience must become integrated before you move on to the next one. This allows you to back up, correct any course deviations, and gain some confidence and momentum.

Be careful what you ask for

At one time in my life, I envisioned how wonderful it would be to live with another family and share cooking and child care duties. I thought it would be nice to live with a family that shared our lifestyle and spiritual and nutritional beliefs.

My dream came true, but not as I imagined it. What I had failed to put into my manifestation was the fact that it would be *our* house.

My husband was purchasing a business in a new city. Due to a predefined deadline, we moved there before the contract was signed. Then the seller—who was going into foreclosure—changed his mind and the deal was off.

Here we were in a new town without jobs or a home. Thank goodness a family opened their spacious home to us. For three months we shared space and responsibilities with people who held the same values as us. Yet it never dawned on me when I was creating this "shared lifestyle" manifestation that it would take place in *someone else's* home.

Ask for what you really desire

Finally, ask for what you really desire. When you have clear intention, it is so much easier to make a movie that will give you what you truly desire. Your movie should always be the highest expression of your heart's desire. If you want money for college, your movie should include a symbol of completion, like seeing a diploma.

When you look for and focus on the highest and most evolved version of your heart's desire, it is easier to manifest, and will often take you out of "solution-mode." Your job is to create the desired outcome—the Universe's job is to fulfill it. Stay in your job. Stay in your joy. The Universe will do the rest.

Summary

Optimize your success in movie making by learning to access favorable states of mind where your emotion is easily accessible. Arouse your good feelings and then use your imagination to fill in the picture.

Your *movie-of-the-mind* can be based on your own past experiences or experiences of superheroes from books, video games, TV shows, or the real movies. You can also use your response to the happy experiences of others if you can emotionally connect to the experience.

You can have non-negotiable items in your movie. It is OK. Treat them like difficult movie stars and know they may slow the speed of your manifestation.

If the leading man or woman in your movie leaves, know there is always someone else waiting to fill the role. Be grateful for what you have received so that the Universe sends more.

Remember, if you cannot imagine it or find some analogy to make it viewable, you will not be able to manifest it. Make your movie believable to you.

Set high goals and be sure to integrate your success. If you find yourself in a self-sabotage situation, examine your actions and thoughts and learn from them. Learn to be patient, recognizing your slow moving manifestations give you mastery.

Be willing to take reasonable risks. Be willing to invest in yourself, but don't get greedy when your ship does come in. If you move in baby steps you will gain mastery faster, because you will learn from your little mistakes and not make big mistakes that will inhibit you from trying again.

Baby steps will take you from playing with paint like a child to being an artist who learns to work with paint to create what he really desires. This is another benefit to having that time lag in your manifestations

Be careful in what you visualize; it may manifest in a way you don't expect if you leave out important details. Ask for what you really desire. When you have clear intention, it is so much easier to make a movie that quickly and easily manifests. If you want money for college, your movie should include a symbol of completion, like seeing a diploma.

Finally, look for and focus on the highest and most evolved version of your heart's desire. Your job is to create the desired outcome—the Universe's job is to fulfill it. Stay in your job. Stay in your joy. The Universe will do the rest.

Chapter 6

Using Fear to Fuel the Genie

Have you ever observed a little child right after he falls down or hurts himself? If the caregiver fails to offer immediate recognition of the situation, the child's response escalates. If the clamor doesn't get attention, the child will get louder still until his needs are recognized.

Yet, if that same child is acknowledged quickly with some form of comfort, soon he will squirm to get away and get back to play. This is like your fear. Pay attention and it dissolves, ignore it and it escalates.

During one of the many moments I was filled with fear about paying my monthly bills, I allowed myself to get a little deeper into the feeling and find out more about the energy of the fear. Maybe I could figure out what the message was. This was during the most financially difficult period of my life, while I was trying to find a way to pay for my son's college and could barely pay the bills with my lowered income and high debt load.

This experience began with my feeling a lot of fear about a utility bill for about $50, which was due that week. As I worried about whether I had enough money in my checking account to cover it, I began to feel really fearful. Although this was a familiar feeling, it seemed to be out of proportion to the fear that I would expect to experience over a $50 utility bill.

I allowed the feeling to sit with me for a moment, and then became aware of a recent purchase. I had bought a fashionable jacket that worked well with my wardrobe—good colors, right size—which was on sale for $50 (1/3 its original cost). This jacket popped into my field of vision, along with the similarly priced utility bill, which I didn't have the funds to pay. I had never made any association between those two events before now. Such a simple "aha" and yet I hadn't noticed it until my fear showed it to me.

My fear was providing important feedback about my actions. In addition, it was also showing me exactly where I was out of integrity with my desire to pay my bills and send my son to college. This fear was showing me how and where I was sabotaging my desire to provide for my family. I understood that my fear was a powerful catalyst in helping me to shore up my actions, and to align them with my desires.

I meet the fear monsters

I began to address my fears as friends, and found out that they had messages for me. Because they were not used to being recognized, or heard, they showed up as raggedy little beings. But just like a mom, I began to talk to them sweetly and see what they had to say. Once I changed my reaction to them they weren't so scary. Pretty soon I began to see them as messengers.

One of the first techniques I discovered to deal with fear is to say, "I love you, little Fear Monsters." (See Figure 6-1) A friend overheard me, and said, "They hate it when you do that," and of course we both burst out laughing! Yet I saw them as unruly little children. All they really needed was a little cleaning up, and I could do that.

Little Fear Monsters
Figure 6-1

I started to see the Fear Monsters as the funky messengers. Those messengers, the Fear Monster Messengers, are going to deliver that parcel whether I am home or not. If you miss the delivery person, they leave a note, and tell you when they will return.

Sometimes it requires several trips and a signature, but the package always gets delivered. My job is to accept the package and thank the messenger.

Fears can express "don't wants"

Some negative thoughts are simply you deciding what you "don't want." This is helpful because it allows you to become clearer about what you *do* desire. Understand that this kind of fear is already clearly labeled. If you were formerly married to an alcoholic and don't want to be married to a spouse who comes home drunk, then your "don't want" leads you to what you do desire.

If you find yourself describing your desires in terms of "don't wants," you must first recognize that this is helpful information, and then rephrase your desire in a form that expresses what you DO desire.

One method is to write one "don't want" item at the top of a page of a spiral notebook. Each page gets a new "don't want" item. Imagine the opposite characteristic that would apply and write it below each negative one. Then list other attributes that you would like to see to define it further. Put the notebook away in a place where you won't see it for a while. When you come across it again you will be pleasantly surprised that your "don't want" list is already taken care of.

For example, under the list "I don't want a partner to come home late." you would list:

> *I desire a partner who comes home on time; who calls when he needs to be late and calls to tell me he misses me when business takes him out of town.*

How your fears operate in the quantum zone

Scary thoughts are energy. These thoughts and feelings are simply energy messages created by you to get your attention. When you allow them to speak they will tell you why they were created in the first place. They are inviting you to see how your thoughts and actions are out of integrity with your desires. Once you acknowledge the message you can move forward. Take a look at a famous quote by General George Patton:

"I never take counsel of my fears."

- US General George Patton

Figure 6-2

What is significant about Patton's remark in Figure 6-2 is that he doesn't allow his fears to rule him. Rather than denying their presence, his statement acknowledges his fears and dismisses them. He knew instinctively what we resist, persists. Patton was hearing the fear messages, and then dismissing them, just like he might dismiss a staff sergeant who came with news that he didn't agree with, or didn't want to hear.

Patton would not dismiss that messenger without first hearing his message. Woe be to a messenger who wouldn't deliver the message, no matter how terrifying it might be. Any member of the military who couldn't get through to Patton would know to go up the chain of command to find someone with more stars or bars to make sure Patton received the message. Fear operates the same way. If the message isn't heard, it escalates.

Can you allow yourself to dismiss your fears after hearing their message? Of course you can! Once they have been heard they will no longer strangle you and keep you from moving forward. Hearing the message is critical. So is heeding the message's *intent*, which is to give you necessary information. *It is your choice* whether you fall prey to believing that the message is a possible outcome or a real scenario. It is all up to you.

Using spheres of influence

In America today, most people receive advertising material that they don't want. When it arrives, you don't judge the person who was paid to deliver it. You simply look at it long enough to determine if it is useful. If you don't want it you don't give it another thought, you just discard it. Remember this the next time you get advice you don't want. Just say, "Thank you." and toss it from your mind. If you express anger or frustration about it, guess what you will get more of?

Dismissing the messenger

Once you dismiss the messenger, don't shoot him. Be aware and stay in your own space, without feeling the need or desire to defend your actions. If you feel defensive, then you are in judgment of yourself or the other person. If you are judging yourself, then discover the source of that inner voice and find out *why* you are judging yourself. It may be that it is a voice from your past. Once you identify the source, you can effectively hear the message and dismiss the judgment.

Fear is a messenger.
Treat it like one.

When the doorbell rings, don't send your fear away without hearing its message.
You wouldn't think of ignoring the mailman or the delivery service.

Figure 6-3

If you are judging someone else, then somewhere in your consciousness, you are not consistent with your beliefs and behaviors. I call this your field of integrity. Many things make up this field—your actions, your words, your beliefs—and they all have to be synchronized for you to be acting in integrity. Make the choice now to allow the other person his or her opinion. Their opinion may be right for them, and when you allow them to hold their beliefs without changing yours, it supports your field of integrity.

Recycling

You can re-use your fear messenger. In many offices where the delivery person brings packages, they may be able to pick up any outbound shipments you have. You may as well put the messenger to work for you. Knowing that fear is energy with a negative charge, you will need to clean it up before you re-use it and send it along with the outbound packages. After you have turned the negative charge into a positive, see yourself taking this "positive emotion" as if it were a ball of energy and toss it into your lighthouse and run your movie.

How do you clean up and change the polarity of your fear?

You do this by inviting the positive intent to surface. First, focus on the feeling of fear. As you feel it, notice how your body feels. Pay attention to how it triggers feelings in your gut, or throat or head. Then calmly address it – as if you were speaking to a friend.

Say something in your thoughts like, "All right, I feel scared, but what is the positive intent behind my fear?" or "I can feel this fear, what is the message?" Once you know the message, ask more questions until the meaning is clear. These can be, "Yes, I understand that but ...?" Sometimes it may take a few moments of quiet and silence after posing your question to get your inner answer. Even if doing this is a stretch for you, give it a try. You will be amazed that you can know the answer to your query!

Once you understand the underlying meaning, you can then look at it for its core value in your reality. If it is showing you that your actions and words don't match your integrity, then you must change. If it turns out to be coming from one of your outer spheres, and you don't share that belief, you can easily dismiss it, because the information runs counter to your inner thoughts about your goals and desires.

For example, if you went shopping yet couldn't pay the bills, and the Fear Monsters show you that you are out of integrity with your desire to pay your bills, you would *decide* to pay bills first, and then shop. If however, you love the color red, and you regret not buying that red jacket that you love so much, you may discover in your memories that your mother had told you, "Redheads don't wear red." It may be that the Fear Monsters' message is coming from your mother's belief about what redheads can wear, and you may choose to change *your* belief. In either case, the emotion that is triggered can be reframed to the positive with your clear intention.

Examining the message and recognizing you are out of integrity is not enough. Do *not* beat yourself up. Instead, make a commitment to yourself to make a **new and different choice** the next time you find yourself in similar circumstances.

While you don't have to return your purchase, you might seriously decide to create a new model for yourself that would make it easier to make the choice that supports your desires. Simply put, get back into integrity and then stay there. Be consistent.

Change your behavior or change your belief

An alternate course of action would be to change your belief system. You always have free will. If your current belief system no longer pleases you, then change your beliefs to line up with your actions. If the fear message is based in reality, you have two choices—either way, you must change—your belief or your behavior.

> "The most convincing way of disputing a negative belief is to show that it is factually incorrect. Much of the time you will have facts on your side, since pessimistic reactions to adversity are so often overreactions."[18]

Everything has an energetic charge. When you acknowledge the message, you have removed the negative emotional charge and you can turn it into a positive, helpful message. In order to recycle and reuse the energy of fear, you must clean it up first. Acknowledging it clears the negative charge; realizing it is helpful and then choosing to change either your belief or behavior reverses it to the positive.

The next step requires visualization. See the now positive emotional energy as a ball of light and toss it into the quantum zone where your lighthouse is located. Then run your manifestation movie. Remember that your emotion is energy you can invest elsewhere. Once you have released the "negative charge," you may use it the same way as your other emotions: to fund your lighthouse and run your movies.

This is one of the most significant tools in the *Genie* work. You will be inviting all the fears in your mind to speak to you, one at a time of course. In the workshop environment, I find that participants often deal with their fears *as if all fears* are valid. All fears are not valid. Discover your fear's message and you will know if it is valid or not. If it is not valid, change your belief about it. If it is valid, change your behavior.

---

[18] Seligman, Martin E. P., *Learned Optimism*, pg. 221, Pocket Books, NY, NY

Mass consciousness beliefs

Working with people over the years, I have found that the feeling of fear has a certain quality that seems to self-perpetuate. Fear is an emotion that is built into our operating system to keep us safe. Some of our fear is coming from mass consciousness, so when we experience fear as an emotion we can tap into the energy of mass consciousness fear without realizing it. Your job is to look at your fear – determine its cause and then do something about it.

Once you know the content of your fear message you can reverse its polarity. Don't judge the messenger and remember to recycle.

Choose your battles

This well-known phrase, attributed to Lao Tzu, drives home a point about the spheres of influence: *Every day in every moment, you choose to accept or reject information.* This data is "feedback." Now that you understand the spheres of influence and feedback, you can be selective about the feedback you will allow into your inner sphere.

Remember that the only "fear messenger" feedback you need to pay attention to is that coming from your *inner* sphere. With practice, you can learn to differentiate your authentic inner voice from the voices of the other spheres. Then all you have to do is access this ability to accept or reject feedback.

Overpowering Mass Consciousness Beliefs

You participate in the collective reality spheres all the time. On occasion, you decide that it serves us to step out of that sphere of influence. It is possible to maintain the integrity of our own sphere so strongly that, in spite of the beliefs of the outer spheres (i.e. other's beliefs), they have no effect on our experience.

Remember that first letter from the college that told me to send them $1,000 a month for my son's tuition? You may recall I could barely make the mortgage and utilities payments. I read the letter and threw it away. I remember laughing out loud—thinking, "Well, *that's* not going to

92

happen!" At the time my mind showed me only two possible choices that letter gave me. Make the mortgage or pay tuition. I ignored the letter as feedback that didn't serve me. Why didn't it serve me? The letter filled me with fear about my survival, and my responsibility to take care of my family.

There had to be another way besides sending his college a monthly check. That's why, by ignoring the letter, I was ignoring feedback that didn't serve me. After tossing it, I checked the "fear" for intent, took note and cleared it, and ran my movie to recycle my fear. In the moment you might not know what to do—except to ignore the feedback that doesn't serve you. However, you will recognize it the moment the solution does present itself.

Summary

Recognize that your fear is a messenger. The messenger expects acknowledgment. Some messages tell you of "don't wants." These are good to know so you can convert them into "desires." Some messages are coming from your inner sphere, others from your outer spheres.

You now have a significant tool to deal with fear. Most of us expend lots of energy avoiding and resisting our fears, thereby failing to hear the message! Remember, one of the most powerful tools in the *Genie* work is **recycling your fear**.

Determine the source of your fear. If it's coming from an outer sphere of influence, then you can release it *without judgment*. Someday you might even feel grateful. Don't shoot the messenger, and stay in your own space, without feeling the need or desire to defend your actions.

If you discover you are defensive, understand that you are judging either the other person or yourself. Maintain your integrity by being OK if someone doesn't agree with you.

If the feedback is coming from your *personal* sphere, then know you must accept it and find the positive intent. Is your fear showing how you are out of integrity? Then either choose a new course of action the next time you're in that situation or change your belief system to align it with your action. This will restore your integrity.

Acknowledge the message and remove its negative charge. Remember to recycle and send the newly cleared positive energy via your intention to fund your lighthouse and run your movie.

Chapter 7

Your Divinity Test

Years ago I had my first Divinity Test. I was really scared back then, and even though I knew everything was going to be OK, I had enough stage fright to feel I might fail. You might have these same fears. It's OK to be afraid, and to feel the fear. Just keep moving forward.

I had manifested my first workshop, had over 100 in attendance at the national trade association the previous year and was invited back the following year at NSFRE (National Society of Fund Raising Executives). Not having done as much "manifesting" work as the previous year, I was doubly worried that maybe my experience the previous year was just a fluke. Actually, I was terrified that because this year had been full of demanding family circumstances, and due to my lack of preparation work, I could make a fool of myself.

I was stressing so much that when I got on the shuttle bus for the convention attendees, I was spreading out my materials and reviewing them once again to make sure it would be a good presentation. I had boarded on the first stop of an empty bus since my hotel was the furthest from the convention site. As the bus shuttled closer and closer to the convention area, it was filling up and I noticed the only seating space on the bus was the one next to me. I quickly gathered my things and made room for anyone who might want to sit. With standing room only, I wasn't surprised when someone got on and inched her way toward me. "May I sit here?" "Of course," I said with a smile. She looked twice at me and grinned. "I know you," she said, "You taught that class I took last year… It made all the difference in the world for me…"

> *If you can keep your head when all about you*
> *Are losing theirs and blaming it on you;*
> *If you can trust yourself when all men doubt you,*
> *But make allowances for their doubting too;*

Sound familiar? The above phrases are the first few lines from a famous poem by Rudyard Kipling, titled "If."[19] Often seen on graduation greeting cards, I discovered it as a child and memorized it because I liked it so much. It sums up your Divinity Test.

It's called reality... "stuff" happens

A Divinity Test is a sudden challenge or obstacle that strikes when you least expect it, just when things were progressing wonderfully and you felt your heart's desire was almost within reach. It will test your resolve and faith in yourself. It may be a surprise when it happens, but you can prepare yourself with the strength and knowledge to adjust and overcome it.

Your Divinity Test is God asking you, **"Do you believe in you, as much as I do?"** It's the part of every manifestation process that *requires* you to claim your abilities to manifest as a divine being. It requires you to step into self-mastery. Facing your Divinity Test is where you **recognize** you are out there all by yourself and decide you must continue.

Do you have faith in you? Remember the venture capitalist discussion in the previous chapter? They won't invest in *any* business unless you, the seeker of funds, are willing to risk your own personal capital as well.

Critical times are your Divinity Tests

The Divinity Test is often overlooked because you don't recognize it for what it is. Have you ever driven down a road when a sudden curve caught you off guard? This is a perfect analogy for the Divinity Test. If you knew the curve was there, it wouldn't be a Divinity Test. When it catches you by surprise you must quickly slow down. If you KNOW there is a curve somewhere ahead, you can be prepared. You watch the signs, then slow down *ahead* of the curve and accelerate through it.

The Divinity Test can take you by surprise because everything is going well and you are happy as you believe you are going to achieve your

---

[19] Kipling, Rudyard, "If". Source: *A Choice of Kipling's Verse* (1943) by T.S. Eliot, Rudyard Kipling

desired outcome! When something happens to shake your belief in your outcome, you are facing your Divinity Test.

The last step before you succeed

When the Columbia space shuttle blew up in the early months of 2003, we were told that the two most critical times for a space shuttle are takeoff and re-entry. In life we hold celebrations for new beginnings but we don't always have a plan for final phase before completion, or re-entry. Re-entry can be compared to the completion of your movie and the imminent attainment of your heart's desire. These critical times are when your Divinity Tests will occur. They are a test of your resolve, persistence and willingness to believe in yourself.

Nature and life are full of examples. We put energy into supporting beginnings. We hold celebrations to support the beginning of cycles—baptisms or naming rites for newborns, graduations, weddings, etc.—but no preparation ceremony for the Divinity Test, the dark before the dawn.

If you *KNOW* the Divinity Test presents some kind of challenge to your resolve and you are prepared for it, it is easier to move through it. Yes, the Universe **is** checking you out to see if you are REALLY serious about your manifestation, and to see if you are really serious about *you*.

FedEx and the very real Frederick Smith

Frederick W. Smith, the man who founded Federal Express,[20] had created his dream and was bankrupt. He had no money, yet he believed his idea would work. Many of you have heard, Mr. Smith was a Yale undergraduate in 1965 which was written about his dream of *a world-wide overnight delivery service*, pulled a C+ grade. His professor commented

---

[20] Smith, Frederick W., Founder, Chairman, President and CEO of Federal Express. The company incorporated in June 1971 and officially began operations on April 17, 1973, with the launch of 14 small aircraft from Memphis International Airport. On that night, Federal Express delivered 186 packages to 25 U.S. cities from Rochester, NY, to Miami, Fla. Through numerous FedEx acquisitions, FedEx has expanded its global presence, now offering services in more than 220 countries and territories, including domestic express services in 18 countries. It has evolved to one of the world's largest corporations, operating in 211 countries, employing over 200,000 people and producing $44.3 billion in total revenues in fiscal year 2013, more than double 2001 revenues.

that "it would never work." He ignored this negative feedback and proceeded to hang on to his dream and eventually start the company and raise the money to create the company we all now know.

However, not many know that on a particular night he had received word from his accounting department that they were broke. They did not have enough to make payroll and the balloon payment on those airplanes. They would be out of business at the end of the week.

Facing that dark night of the soul, the Divinity Test

Smith was already extended as far as his investors could support. Yet, he was really clear about his business and that it would succeed. He did two things. He asked all his employees to cash their checks at the grocery store instead of the bank. This would give him an extra two days of float. This was long before automatic (direct) deposit. He took all the cash he could pull together and boarded one of his planes to Las Vegas. He played in the casino and won really big that night. He won enough money to cover the company's payroll obligations and keep his company going until it was solvent. He quit playing that night as soon as he reached the needed sum.

What are you to do?

I don't recommend gambling or making risky ventures. I do recommend you explore all possibilities to fulfill your heart's desire. Sometimes just saying to yourself, "There has got to be a solution to this situation, and *I choose to discover it*," will open you to a solution you had not considered or known previously. Keep your integrity, and please – keep it legal.

Your Divinity Test

After you have told the Universe this is your outcome and you will accept nothing less, let it be. Don't go into the emotion of grief about your failure! If you do that, you will have seeded the quantum zone with your new (sad) emotion and new visual which will surely affect the outcome.

Instead, remain mystified as to why the "apparent" data gives you a failure notice. Remain in *wonder*. When you are in a Divinity Test, trust that you have within you the knowledge of the next step or that it is forthcoming.

This inner awareness makes room for the ideas to present themselves and helps you maintain your dream and claim your outcome.

There must be a mistake!

Your dream must have such clarity that you can say to yourself, "I will not walk away. I believe in my dream; I will accept the incoming data that supports my heart's desire and discard everything else." There will be enough data to support what you know to be real and true in your reality. The rest will follow.

Frederick Smith knew he had a viable business because he had already received enough support in the business community. He just needed a little extra boost to get through that Divinity Test.

Another wonderful book full of Divinity Tests is a book by Barbara Stanny called "Secrets of Six Figure Women."[21] A good read, it is a handy companion to help you stay in the present and achieve your outcome. The author reminds you, when that moment of doubt comes in, surrender is a pretty good choice of action. I believe this is true, and is part of the process of "allowing" the Universe to fill in the blank and create or show you a solution that had not been visible to you.

Lessons from Geese

Written by Angeles Arrien, for the 1991 Organizational Development Network, and based on the work of Milton Olson, this lovely set of five facts about geese (see below) emphasizes the value in working together, the pitfalls of pulling out of formation, the need to assist one who falls, the taking of turns with the big jobs, and the offering of praise to one another in the form of honking.

---

[21] Stanny, Barbara, *Secrets of Six-Figure Women: Surprising Strategies to Up Your Earnings and Change Your Life.*

Lessons from Geese

Fact 1:
As each goose flaps its wings it creates an "uplift" for the birds that follow. By flying in a "V" formation, the whole flock adds 71% greater flying range than if each bird flew alone.

Lesson:
People who share a common direction and a sense of community can get where they are going quicker and easier because they are traveling on the thrust of one another.

Fact 2:
When a goose falls out of formation, it suddenly feels the drag and resistance of flying alone. It quickly moves back into formation to take advantage of the lifting power of the bird immediately in front of it.

Lesson:
If we have as much sense as a goose, we stay in formation with those headed where we want to go. We are willing to accept their help and give our help to others.

Fact 3:
When the lead goose tires, it rotates back into the formation and another goose flies to the point position.

Lesson:
It pays to take turns doing the hard tasks and sharing leadership. As with geese, people are interdependent on each other's skills, capabilities and unique arrangements of gifts, talents or resources.

Fact 4
The geese flying in formation honk to encourage those up front to keep up their speed.

Lesson:
We need to make sure our honking is encouraging. In groups where there is encouragement, the production is much greater. The power of encouragement (to stand by one's heart or core values and encourage the heart and core of others) is the quality of honking we seek.

Fact 5
When a goose gets sick, wounded or shot down, two geese drop out of formation and follow it down to help and protect it. They stay with it until it dies or is able to fly again. Then, they launch out with another formation or catch up with the flock.

Lesson:
If we have as much sense as geese, we will stand by each other in difficult times as well as when we are strong.

Follow the buddy system

Following the example of Lessons from Geese, one of the best ways to prepare for the Divinity Test is to have a buddy to whom you can turn in your moment of self-doubt. Let the buddy reflect to you what he or she has already seen you accomplish. This is a very powerful tool that will assist you in moving through your Divinity Test very quickly. I highly recommend the buddy system.

Amazingly, a study of the air currents created by geese flying in formation produces Phi ratios. Coincidence? Hardly! Not too long ago, aircraft manufacturers Aerbus of France and Boeing in the USA announced a joint venture to develop jets that would allow for this same close flying in formation to capitalize on the 70% fuel savings that could be gained while crossing the Atlantic.

The following "Lessons from Geese" was transcribed from a speech given by Angeles Arrien at the 1991 Organizational Development Network and was based on the work of Milton Olson.

Discerning a Divinity Test from a message to give up

How do you tell the difference between the Divinity Test and a message from the Universe that says "give up"? You don't want to end up like the fabled Man of La Mancha chasing the "Impossible Dream."

The Universe supports your creation because that is the job of the Universe. It's your job to create. It's not possible for the Universe to deny you. You may unintentionally send mixed signals to the Universe. You might YoYo from desiring something, then fearing it, back and forth you go. When that happens you may get a "stop work" order from the Universe. This is only a temporary work stoppage until you get more *clarity* about your manifestation. When you stop sending mixed signals, the "work of manifesting" resumes.

Synchronicities prove your manifestation is "cooking"

A true Divinity Test will be supported by synchronicities. If you pay attention, you will see that even when **you** have self-doubt, the Universe is sending you signals that you are on the path to achieving your goal. These synchronicities will be situational coincidences that tell you "You are on track." "Keep going." "You can do this." It is incumbent that you to recognize and claim your "go ahead" signal.

One of my students, JoAnne Jewel, tells the story of her desire to move out West. She had to leave her family and friends behind to fulfill her heart's desire. She knew she must, but was torn at the prospect. Actually, she was pretty darned scared to leave everything familiar to go live in a new place by herself.

The next time she went to see her doctor, she let him know she was going to move out West. He asked exactly where in Northern California was her desired destination. Earlier in the week she had visited her lawyer. He too had asked, "Where are you going in California?" She had only said she was "going out West."

Neither her doctor nor her lawyer knew her intended destination, yet both men gave her the remarkable *synchronicity* of her decision to move to Northern California. Both men were messengers from the Universe telling her to believe in herself and the new location that she had been called to.

Why the Divinity Test?

The purpose of the Divinity Test is to find out if you believe in you. The Universe wants you to be certain. Passing your Divinity Test is a way to express your belief in you when "everyone around you is losing their heads and blaming it on you..." Knowing about The Divinity Test is a way to be ready to own your belief that you *are* a co-creator with God. Passing the test proves it.

Training wheels

If you know the Universe is going to test your resolve, and you are firm, you will sail through the Divinity Test safely. You usually shore up your energies very easily when you are going into something new, being very aware that as you begin something you must prepare for it.

Very often we overlook the part of the cycle that takes us up to the final win or to mastery. We might be cruising along nicely and not even realize that there is a big curve in the road, or that some major level of support

102

will be withdrawn. Plan for the moment when your training wheels are removed. Knowing about the Divinity Test allows you to plan for it.

Don't settle

Donald Trump, in *The Art of the Deal,*[22] writes about being extremely passionate about each deal, no matter what it is. At the same time, he states he is willing to walk away at any time if it doesn't meet his minimum standard. You can too.

This is an important element that will help you define a fork in the road. Your goal is to have passionate "attached detachment." Yet it is a bit of a conundrum to be expected to desire something passionately and yet be willing to walk away.

Giving yourself permission to have something includes being clear about what you desire and the minimums you will accept, and recognizing that you don't have to settle for something that fails to meet your standard.

Accepting the "almost" perfect doesn't serve you. If this occurs, let go and stay in gratitude. If you are shopping for the perfect sweater that must match a pair of trousers, you don't return home with an almost match, you keep looking! Your dreams, goals and manifestations deserve the same respectful treatment.

Don't be afraid to reject an outcome that is close, but missing an important element. If it is missing a **minor** element, and you don't mind if your heart's desire comes in missing that minor element, then accepting it is your choice. If you Higher Self tells you to accept the minor defect, go with it, as it may lead you to something better down the road.

When an outcome is close to providing what you really desire, another version of your heart's desire is moving in right behind it. This next version will be a closer fit than the one before it. The Phoenix Sequence helps you understand why.

---

[22] Trump, Donald J. and Schwartz, Tony, *Trump: The Art of the Deal,* (Dec 28, 2004)

Look for the Phoenix Sequence

Stay tuned, because in Chapter 14, the **Phoenix Sequence** is explained in great detail. We think it will knock your socks off.

We expect the *Phoenix Sequence* will give you a very exciting "aha" moment when we show you what nature can prove and you can use. Sacred geometry is found everywhere, as you have probably heard from many sources. The symmetry and order in the Universe continues to delight and astound us. Consider this often-used quote:

> *[The scientist's] religious feeling takes the form of a rapturous amazement at the harmony of natural law, which reveals and intelligence of such superiority, that in comparison with it, all the systematic thinking of human beings is an utterly insignificant reflection.*[23] - Albert Einstein

In Part II of this book, *The Principles & Proofs*, we show through a simple exercise how sacred geometry will take you beyond that moment of doubt, which then allows you to focus on your manifestation confidently.

Once you realize that each expression of the Golden Mean brings you closer and closer to the mathematical ideal of this ratio, it allows you to recognize and comprehend that Phi, or the Golden Mean, **is** Source Code of the Universe. You then can see how it relates to your ideal outcome from where you are, and takes you to the point beyond belief to *knowing*. This is why using sacred geometry to manifest is so profound. It becomes irrefutable.

Knowing occurs because we mathematically show you why and how each version of your manifestation hovers near your ideal outcome. If one result *seems* perfect, but fails to deliver on one important element, you can easily let go and know that another one is on the way. You then stay in gratitude and run your movie often.

---

[23] Einstein, Albert, *The World as I See It*, Secaucus, New Jersey: The Citadel Press, 1999, pp. 24-29

Practical applications

My sons learned at a very young age about manifestation. For years, one of them talked about buying my car from me. I liked my car so much that I wasn't ready to give it up by the time he was ready to buy one. He told his father he wanted "the same car" that mom had.

His father located a car that was just like mine, except it had an automatic transmission. My son told his father he would buy it, even though it wasn't exactly what he had in mind.

A week later, another car, exactly like the one my son wanted—including a stick shift, manual transmission—came on the market. His father purchased this one for himself. If my son had waited another week, or had turned down the first car, the really perfect car would have been his!

Recognizing your Divinity Test

Very often your Divinity Test is so strong and powerful that all available data says you won't make it. Sometimes a business or romantic partner may let you down or withdraw from a contract. This withdrawal means you aren't going to get your outcome with *that* person. It doesn't mean you won't have your outcome, like so many people might think. Make room for a new way to see this.

You may find yourself arguing internally. Your personal *sphere of influence* and the outer spheres that represent the 3-D physical reality might be in disagreement because the obvious partner has bowed out. But you should continue to see the possibilities here.

Stay with your outcome!

It is also imperative that you give yourself permission to express your feelings of grief, pain, disappointment and disillusionment enough to get it out of your system. Give yourself a limited amount of grieving time. Honor the human emotions around loss, but don't stop there. Give yourself a brief "good cry." Tell your story once or twice, but no more than three times. My company even has an AroMandalas® Essential Oil Blend, *Passages*,[24] which will help you move through your grief quickly.

The secret Phoenix formula

The more you "seed" the Universe with your grief, the more watered down your manifestation matrix will be. With your grief uppermost in your mind, you may forget to run your movie. Emotions such as these will slow down your process. If you ignore your sadness, and the normal expression of grief, it will get worse because what you resist, persists! Find the middle ground.

Look for the fork in the road

This is a classic opportunity to see yourself with the success you had in mind, regardless of your partner or the situation. On a mental timeline, go back to the fork in the road where the former partner joined you. Take a new direction from this point forward imagining a new and different partner who does proceed to the finish line with you. This is another version of how your heart's desire scenario might play out. The new inner technologies I'm using will show you that you can hold two versions of the reality at the same time. Like watching two movies simultaneously, you don't force yourself to believe one over the other.[25]

When you purposefully allow more than one version of the reality to exist (the disappointing one with the former partner and the new one) you offer no resistance to the Universe. This is good. In the next chapter (Chapter 8) you will learn about *energy dominance*. The Universe energizes the version with the most energy (positive or negative) with more of the same. What **do** you want? By deciding to curtail the "excessive negative emotion" around the (sad) version that you "don't want," it floods your positive outcome with more energy, ensuring your *Genie* manifestation.

---

[24] AroMandalas.com, *Passages*. This essential oil blend will help you let go of big emotions and move through sadness and grief. AroMandalas® *Passages* blend supports you when dealing with closed doors, presenting you with windows of opportunity. AroMandalas® Essential Oil Blends are offered exclusively through Transformational Enterprises, Inc. at http://www.AroMandalas.com.
[25] FlowerofLifeblog.com, "Merlin Mysteries" by Maureen St. Germain, September, 2013

Sometimes all you need to pass your Divinity Test is a little patience and perspective. When you look at something too closely, too often, all of the conflicting information will keep you from getting an accurate view of the prevailing direction.

Version two

In this version of your movie, you start from a time where you took a different path, one that ensures your heart's desire. This alternate path includes your being with an *unspecified* partner. You do not need to know who the person is to believe the perfect partner has appeared.

See yourself with the heart's desire you had in mind, regardless of your partner or situation. If done correctly, your movie's visual image included this partner as a faceless person, so it won't matter who he or she is. You can still use the good feelings and sweet memories (from the former partner) as emotional energy without having a specific person's face in mind.

This is where that statement, **"I don't care what everyone else says or thinks, I am going to have my outcome."** bears repetition and will serve you very well. If that former partner is going to participate, he or she will move to catch up with you. If not, someone else will.

Perspective and patience

If you were royalty—and you are—you would think nothing of sending the wrong meal back to the chef. "There must be some mistake," you might say to the waiter. Then you would insist the right meal be served and wait for it.

Conflicting reports

If you over-examine every turn in the road, you may discover that you aren't going the direction you intended, and then you may panic and turn around! Oops! If you allow yourself some wiggle room and look at the big picture, you will see that all is well. This is why they tell investors in the stock market to use a "long-term" strategy and to plan on waiting several years for the growth in value.

Compass directions

A person traveling across country from east to west may have a compass in the car. This person is also following the road signs. The driver could actually be on a road that says "west" while his compass is pointing east. What's going on here? The road may divert around a mountain or lake, which cannot be crossed in the desired direction.

Even though your compass may tell you that you are traveling in the opposite direction you wish to go, you know to trust the road signs. You know that eventually the road will take you in the direction you wish to go. **So trust the signs**, and ignore feedback that looks at every little detail to see if it supports your outcome. Invest in your heart's desire with a "long-term" strategy.

Every little detail will not support your *Genie* manifestation. However, as long as you have some large form of confirmation, like road signs, or the doctor and lawyer in the above story, your *synchronicities*, you can be confident of your *Genie* Movie's outcome. Remember, allow the Universe to determine "how" to fulfill your heart's desire.

Gerry's Law of Change

When my children were young, I shared with my mother how proud I was that one of my sons who had been particularly challenging to raise was showing signs of maturity. He had made great progress in growing up and I told her how much that meant to me.

My mother cautioned me, saying, "Just about the time that you think your son is mature, he will do something really stupid. Kids don't grow up in a straight line." I think my mother was right, not only about kids, but also about all kinds of change.

Change does not occur in a straight line. If you chart change (Figure 7-1), you will discover there are forward steps and backward steps, then more forward movement and then some backsliding. This process continues until the change moves above the desired line, which represents your outcome, and stays there. I decided to name this law of change after my mom, Gerry.

Gerry's Law of Change

**The straight line indicates the desired change.
The jagged line shows the progress, and the dips,
for each cyclic adjustment you make.**

Figure 7-1

Day traders use law of change

In one of my *Genie* workshops, a day trader friend looked at my chart of change and said, "That is the same chart they use to track changes in the stock market!" What a coincidence!

Gerry's Law of Change is identical to one used by traders using a system based on sacred geometry. For a trader, the ideal is to have the stock prices hover the same distance above and below the line. It looks like a graph (a sine wave) of the computation of Phi as produced from a Phoenix Sequence! (See Chapter 14)

The gray straight line in the drawing is the goal line. Your progress is the jagged black line. As you can see from this chart, the changes you make give you some success right away. Then you slip back into your old habits and behaviors. As you reapply yourself to make changes you make another big leap.

For each level of success you experience a little slippage. Each time you cycle through, you discover you are further along on the continuum than before.

When you are training and tracking your input, while running your movie with the energy from both positive and negative emotions,[26] you will be able to easily manage these little drops in your perceived outcome. Understand and accept that as you move forward and find your new center point, your patterns will hover around the goal line.

It may *feel* like your apparent backward movement is increasing; however, what is really happening is that you are becoming more familiar with the newness, and every deviation from it seems larger than before. If you stay focused and keep running your movie in times of doubt, you will be fine.

Show us your suitcase – again

While waiting one time at the Kona, Hawaii, airport, having cleared the agricultural inspection, security inspection and then the carry-on inspection, I noticed one more sign for the agricultural inspection of carry-on luggage. The sign said, "Yes, you do have to do this again." Yes, you may go through your Divinity Test many times.

Volunteering for your Divinity Test

You can step up to the plate and take one of your Divinity Tests ahead of time. Volunteering for a Divinity Test is sometimes a lot easier and really moves your manifestation work along.

Back in 1993, I attended an introductory class on what has become known as the Flower of Life (FOL) workshop. I was enchanted. Here was a class that covered all the esoteric concepts and ideas I had been studying for the past twenty years.

I decided to become a facilitator of this knowledge. When someone attending the same class as me asked what it would take to become a facilitator, the workshop leader said they weren't training any more facilitators. I ignored his response. I disregarded the negative feedback with a mental thought, "That does not apply to me."

---

[26] Using negative emotions is found in Chapter 6, "Using Fear to Fuel the Genie."

When I attended my first full FOL workshop, there was a woman who had already taken the facilitator training and was now attending her second FOL class. When I inquired why she would repeat this class, she informed me that her facilitator certification would not be complete until she had attended the workshop a second time.

I don't care what everyone else says or thinks, I am going to have my outcome.

Equipped with this new information, I decided to repeat the Flower of Life workshop the following February knowing that if they ever opened up the training, I would have fulfilled this requirement. Both the time and the funds had been easily provided for me to do this. When I registered, the facilitator asked me why I was taking the class a second time. "Didn't you get it?" he asked.

I really didn't want to hear his response or participate in this conversation. I knew what he would say and did not wish to accept his version about the facilitator program. I answered nonchalantly, "Yes, I understood the material." He persisted. I finally stated to him, "It is my intention to become a FOL facilitator."

He, of course, responded with the same information he had told the first lady at the introductory lecture I had attended. Upon hearing it, I replied, "That is YOUR reality, I choose another." It helps to have some prepared statements for those moments when someone else is certain that he or she is right. Other people are right, in *their* reality.

That fall the founder, Drunvalo Melchizedek, held a facilitator training, even though months earlier it was "never going to be offered again." The Universe provided many miracles to make sure I would be there, in spite of some pretty impressive obstacles.

I had planned, with my sister, to celebrate her birthday and our mother's 70th birthday over the Thanksgiving holiday. Both my mom and sister each sent me $100 to make sure I had travel fare for this special occasion. Although this might not seem like much, it was a big sign for someone with serious cash problems.

Three months earlier, when I was hired at my new job, I had told them there might be a training that I was interested in – and would need to take time off if it opened up and I was accepted. I went to my boss to explain the situation and she graciously found a way for me to attend so that I didn't have to lose any pay–even though the rules didn't allow for this.

I was able to book the ticket to my sister's house (in one city in Arizona) to attend the family celebration, then fly to the next city (also in Arizona), where the training was held and then home. The cost for the extra stop was just a few dollars more than the round-trip ticket for the family gathering. For me it was a miracle.

I believe my clear intent—coupled with absolute faith—in taking the pre-requisite enabled the Universe to let me "take the Divinity Test in advance." My Test was in signing up for and attending a pre-requisite second FOL workshop, even though I didn't know if I would ever be able to make use of it.

But be aware that volunteering for a Divinity Test does not mean that a surprise test won't still occur.

Summary

You cannot always predict when the Divinity Test will occur, but you can anticipate it. Very likely it will come when you least expect it, especially at a critical time. It may surprise you, but knowing the signs will enable you to pay attention and pass your Divinity Test.

The Universe will support your creation and a true Divinity Test will be supported by synchronicities. These synchronicities will be situational coincidences that tell you "You are on the right track."

If you have someone specific in mind for your manifestation and he or she drops out, you can simply replace him or her with a faceless partner. You go back to the point in your life before the partner showed up. Begin your manifestation from that point.

Take the time to pound on a pillow, cry, work with AroMandalas *Passages* Blend, feel your rage – and then be done. Avoid *seeding* your

Universe with too much grief. If you *revel in your misery* you will dilute your magic, and dilute the magnet of your manifestation formula.

Let the details be. When you look at something too closely, too often you can get conflicting information. Learn to be patient. Stay focused. Look at every diversion as an opportunity to gain patience. For example, you keep seeing how certain things don't seem to be working out, yet, at the same time, you get a synchronicity event that is solid encouragement, you can be sure you are on the road to success. Look at the synchronistic confirmation and ignore the little stuff that bothers you.

The Phoenix continuum, vibrating back and forth over an imaginary line moving closer and closer, but never actually landing on it, is like Gerry's Law of Change. Gerry's Law says to expect backsliding and challenges. These are normal. Anticipating a fallback doesn't mean that you will have one. But if you do, you will be glad you were prepared.

Volunteering for a Divinity Test is sometimes easier and can move your manifestation work along. Remember, there will be many Divinity Tests ahead. If you can choose when to take some of your tests, you may be better prepared to pass them.

When your Divinity Tests come, how will you respond? Passing your Divinity Tests requires that you decide to keep at it, even though everyone around you may have left your side. It is God asking you "Are you serious about this?" The Divinity Test asks if you are ready to believe in *you* as much as the Creator does.

Chapter 8

Resistance, Resonance and Feedback

Bad things that happen

At age 9, Muhammad Ali received a bicycle for his birthday. One day he parked it outside a gym. When he returned the bicycle was gone, stolen. Someone told him to find a policeman. "I'll find the guy who stole my bike and beat him up," a young Ali told the officer. The policeman found that Ali, then Cassius Clay, didn't know how to fight and offered to teach him to box. He never found the bike or the thief. But Ali did become the World Heavyweight Boxing Champion three times, in 1964, 1974 and 1978.

Al Hirt, the trumpet player famous for his tremendous lungpower, tells a similar story while growing up in New York City. His father saved and saved to purchase a trumpet for him. Finally, the coveted trumpet was his. On the way to school one day, a gang of kids beat him up and bent his trumpet. He straightened it out and never told anyone. He continued to play the trumpet even though the bending and straightening had made a little hole in his horn. The rest is history.

What you resist, persists. The Universe will give you more of the substance or thing you give your attention to. The more you resist or complain about what you don't desire, the more of it you will receive. Be aware of the whining you may be doing in your head. (This was discussed extensively in Chapter 4, "Choice.")

If the same "bad" things keep happening to you, and you are getting more and more frustrated by the minute, consider the possibility that you aren't getting the message. Lessons are learned in spirals. You may "remember" learning some aspect of something before, but this time it has a different element to it. Look for the benefit.

Bless the event

Choose to bless every event. If you find yourself resistant to blessing an event that you are particularly angry or upset about, you can expect more of the same. Instead, choose to "open your heart." Closing your heart closes off possibilities. You might miss the deeper meaning because you accept "this is how things are," rather than seeing "this is a growth opportunity." There is always a benefit to every bad thing that happens. Your job is to look for and find it.

The best course of action is to look at your resistance and find out what is going on. Each of us has had numerous opportunities to experience resistance and to choose differently. It isn't always easy, but with practice, you will be able to use your resistance to help you decide how to live your life. Optimally, resistance keeps you on target. Another benefit is that it helps you hone your persistence skills.

The four kinds of resistance

There are four kinds of resistance. The first kind of resistance is envy. You want what someone else has, and you think you should have it. In this form you know what the resistance is, but stubbornness keeps you stuck. Usually you get an insight or a friend may help you become aware of your envy.

When you become aware, you can let go of those feelings easily by understanding that the world is full of opportunity. You can go right to your outcome unconcerned about anyone else or his or her reality. Please understand that envy implies that there isn't enough to go around. Quantum mechanics shows us we live in a world of all possibilities. If there isn't enough, it is only because we haven't been asking for it.

The second kind of resistance is subtler. You can feel the resistance but at first you don't realize what your feelings are based on. In other words, you don't know that you know, and you are stuck. You may even deny you are resisting anything, but with a little nudging it becomes clear and you are able to shift and adjust. Another way to look at it is that you expect others to change, but you are not willing to do the same.

The third form of resistance is a deep level of resistance that is rooted in some earlier life experience that caused you to make a decision about "the way things are." This "version of reality" no longer serves you. Nor does it exist. Typically, this version of reality taught you some special skill. Now that you have mastered this skill, you no longer need to hold this belief. Once the knowledge is gained, the resistance is no longer necessary.

Perhaps as a child you learned it wasn't safe to express anger, due to an alcoholic parent's explosive temper. You learned to conceal your anger, and now have trouble expressing your true feelings of dissatisfaction in any situation.

Until you learn when to control your anger, and when to express it, you will probably have some dysfunctional relationships. Most relationships rely on clear communication. Learning that extreme anger is unsafe is one thing, but resisting expressing any form of dissatisfaction will ultimately destroy relationships.

You can ask your angels to help you reconnect to that circumstance in your past and bring your present-day wisdom to it. See it from a new perspective. This action will disperse the resistance. In fact, the angels tell me that any time you are willing to ask their help, they will help you disperse your resistance. There is Quantum Matrix healing that I wrote about in the book, *Reweaving the Fabric of your Reality.*[27] You can have someone do this work for you, or you can learn it and work with a friend. Check our website for details on this amazing tool, nicknamed QMH.

The fourth form of resistance is the most painful. It expresses in total denial. You won't believe others when they try to tell you. This is like the woman who was upset with her friend telling her that her idea of the perfect car (a Jeep Cherokee) might not make her happy.

Denial is different from a healthy belief in you. These "don't know that you don't know" aspects are the last part of your ego that you will leave behind in order to manifest your heart's desire. Anytime you are presented

---

[27] MaureenStGermain.com, *Reweaving the Fabric of your Reality*, www.ReweavingtheFabricofyourReality.com

with repeated resistance over the same issue it is a signal that you are in the deepest stage of resistance.

This resistance is based on a deep-rooted fear of lack in your life. The good news is, once you learn to step beyond your ego, the strength you have developed through your ego can be used to hold your sphere of influence. See if you can discover what frightens you. Perhaps you are seeking the familiar, even though it is painful. It is then up to you and your angels to ponder this perception of reality. All you have to do is being willing to see things differently.

Discover the blessing

The movie industry predicted doom and gloom when VCRs first became available. People were going to be able to watch movies at home easily. The movie industry predicted a drop in the movie going public. The exact opposite occurred and movie attendance actually increased.

Find out what doom and gloom **you** are predicting and then look at it from a new vantage-point. Bless every event and discover its benefits.

Cells and feedback

Biology gives us yet another example of nature's use of feedback. There is a dynamic relationship between the receptors of your hormones and hormones that are either ingested or manufactured in the body. For example, Marla Ahlgrimm states about a woman's body that, "during her menstrual cycle, when estrogen rises and peaks, her production of estrogen receptors also increases, in turn increasing her body's ability to respond to the estrogen. This is 'called up-regulation of the receptors.'"[28]

If you saw the movie *What the Bleep?*,[29] you observed yet another researcher's conclusion of a similar biological function. The movie graphically shows how receptors increase their capacity when they get more stimulation, thus causing the body to seek more stimulation of the

---

[28] Ahlgrimm, Marla, *The HRT Solution*, page 31.
[29] *What the Bleep?* was conceived and its production funded by William Arntz, who co-directed the film along with Betsy Chasse and Mark Vicente. All three were students of Ramtha's School of Enlightenment:
 http://en.wikipedia.org/wiki/Ramtha%27s_School_of_Enlightenment.

same sort! It shows a significant biological feedback mechanism can become self-perpetuating.

Optimism can be learned

In his book "Learned Optimism", author Martin E.P. Seligman, Ph.D., tells us that not only can optimism be learned, but that pessimists breed more pessimism in their mind and that optimists bring more optimism to their thinking. This translates into real, tangible results that have been proven scientifically. The optimists have more opportunity offered to them and the pessimists have less.[30]

> *It is important to see the difference between this approach (learned optimism) and the so called 'power of positive thinking'. "Positive thinking often involves trying to believe upbeat statements such as "every day, in every way, I am getting better and better" in the absence of evidence, or even in the fact of contrary evidence. If you can actually believe such statements, more power to you. Many educated people, trained in skeptical thinking, cannot manage this kind of boosterism. Learned optimism, in contrast, is about accuracy.[31]*

Pessimists tend to overdramatize and focus on the negative events that occur. Learned optimism invites the individual to look for and find facts that support the optimistic view.

The most convincing way of disputing a negative belief is to show that it is factually incorrect. Much of the time you will have facts on your side, since pessimistic reactions to adversity are so often overreactions. You adopt the role of a detective and ask, "What is the evidence for this belief?" This nature driven feedback mechanism supports the concept that the more optimism you produce, the more you will produce receptors that will support that optimism.

---

[30] "Pessimism is self-fulfilling. Pessimists don't persist in the face of challenges, and therefore fail more frequently – even when success is attainable." Seligman, Martin E.P., *Learned Optimism*, page 113, Pocket Books, NY, NY 1992

[31] Ibid.

Contract with the Universe

What is in a contract with the Universe? You are assured that you don't have to rely on any one source to cover your income; something is always on its way to you. The Universe will supply a steady source of all you require and desire as long as you show up and do your part.

What does it mean to have a contract with the Universe? It means that instead of looking at your employer or your job as your source of funds, you allow yourself to think in terms of the Universe being your employer. It means that as long as you are willing to show up, the Universe will take care of the rest. After all, you work for a Universe with its endless supply of goodwill and energy.

Everyone has a contract with the Universe. I haven't always known this. I had been leading workshops for almost five years when I discovered I had a contract with the Universe. Sometimes I held a class with as few as two or three people, because I wanted to "keep the flow" going. But here was a first; I was being asked for a refund.

My enrollee, Tom, informed me that a friend of his was hosting the same workshop as mine, but given by someone else. Her workshop was scheduled for the month before the one Tom had registered with me. Tom said that he wanted to support his friend. Yet he had committed to my workshop, which had been scheduled months earlier. Now he wanted me to return his deposit.

I didn't know how to handle it. I said to him, "I've never been asked this before. Would it be all right if I think about it?"

"Of course," he replied, "I will probably take the workshop at my friend's house even if you don't give me the refund."

I wanted to know who the other facilitator was. It was someone I knew and admired. "Wow," I thought, "I would really like this facilitator to think highly of me. I think very highly of him." Well, then it was an easy decision.

It was easy to decide to give a refund this time. Then it occurred to me that it really shouldn't matter who the other facilitator was. The "why's" and "who's" shouldn't matter either. I realized I could apply *this* experience globally to every refund. From that point forward, I made a decision to refund tuition if I was asked for it before class deadlines. I still practice this policy for workshops.

The next time was a little tougher. It was probably a Divinity Test. In this request, two people—a husband and wife—wanted a full refund. With my cash flow issues, sending someone $554 was a very big deal. But I had promised myself that I would provide a refund if someone asked for it.

As I pondered this situation, I was able to recall what was going on when they had registered. The timing of their check coincided with my asking the Universe for the funds for me to attend a specific workshop. I realized that I had used their tuition money to register for a workshop that was important to me.

At the time of their registration there was no extra money for the workshop I wanted to take, but when their check came in I was able to sign up. Now I could see they had made a loan to me when I had needed it, courtesy of the Universe. At this juncture I began to see that I might not have a contract with a specific employer, but that I did have a contract with the Universe.

There is no lack. The Universe supplies abundantly. If you practice this principle when someone wants something, then that is perfectly all right. There's more where it came from. You are well provided for because you have a contract with the Universe. You may as well exercise your options.

What does it mean to have a contract with the Universe? It means that you trust the Universe to supply you with opportunities to fund your life, and that all you have to do is show up and do your part.

When one customer goes away, it's a job that goes away. It doesn't mean that now you will have less, it means that you are making room for more in your life. You can use my experiences to save you the time and trouble I have experienced in learning about abundance. You can receive the benefit without going through what I did.

The end of the story is the best part. I received a call from a woman who wanted to register for the very next class. She was bringing her son to take the class as well. It turned out to be the daughter and grandson of the man who had been given the first refund. I just received two for one!

Later that summer I held an advanced class and *all* three of them took it. That same year this same man signed up for all our workshops. The synchronicity is very profound. This was the Universe teaching me about my contract.

You have a contract with the Universe. You are a free agent. Exercise your options!

What is in Contract with the Universe?

- ✓ *The assurance that you don't rely on any one source to cover your income. The Universe will supply all you require and desire.*
- ✓ *The recognition that you have a steady source of supply coming from the Universe.*
- ✓ *The assurance that something is always on its way to you.*
- ✓ *The requirement that you must show up and do your part.*

What does it mean to have a contract with the Universe? It means that instead of looking at my employer or my job as my source of funds, I allow myself to think in terms of the Universe being my employer. It means that as long as I am willing to show up, the Universe takes care of the rest. After all, I work for a Universe with an endless supply of goodwill and energy.

Figure 8-1

Imagine

Most individuals have some familiarity with John Lennon's famous song, "Imagine." It is one of the world's most popular peace songs. It also invites us to imagine what peace would be like. John understood this principle of imagining an outcome. He taught it in his song, and he practiced it with the Beatles. From his biography:

> *I always knew I was going to make it, but I wasn't sure in what manifestation. I used to read the reviews of books and art and music before I ever put anything out and I'd half expect to see my name in the review, even though I hadn't written a book or song. I was half expecting to see myself in the newspapers, to be famous; I knew it was just a matter of time.* - John Lennon

A friend of John's in New York tells the rest of the story. When the Beatles were beginning their performing career, they were touring all over Europe in a van. After each show John would always drive and lead the group in a little chant. He would ask the question, "Where are we going?" The group's response was always the same, "Straight to the top." He always followed with, "What will we find when we get there?" "Fame and fortune!" came the excited response.

They repeated this over and over as they drove to their place of abode for the night. This friend says John told him, "We forgot to include *happiness.*"

If you decide you want to use this little exercise, you might include the following rewrite: Where are you going? *"Straight to the top."* What will you find when you get there? *"Fame, fortune, flexibility, fun and fulfillment."*

Feedback and integrity

Your parents or parental figures gave you everything you needed in order to be successful. They taught you either to accept or to reject feedback fully. And they also taught you choice. The very act of accepting or rejecting parental feedback caused you to make a choice. Sometimes you learned that a choice we made wasn't "safe" so you choose to never make that choice again!

The classic example of parental training of a child to accept or reject feedback is the parent calling to the child, "Put a coat on. It's cold outside. You'll catch a cold." The child emphatically calls back, "No, I won't." And the child runs off. This child doesn't catch a cold.

The child who *thought* he should put a coat on but didn't will be more likely catch a cold. The child who owns the statement, "No, I won't" is less likely to get sick. When you hold your personal sphere of influence, you maintain your own integrity so strongly that any others cannot influence it.

Perhaps the single most difficult thing you must learn to do is to maintain your personal sphere of integrity.[32] You may be so accustomed to looking to others for feedback that you cannot comprehend life without getting someone else's opinion and approval. You may not realize how dependent you are on this feedback. Whose approval do you need? Why? Be sure the approval you are seeking aligns with your personal beliefs and is not some outer authority dictating from afar.

You may habitually accept feedback indiscriminately and be unsuspecting when you accept it into your personal sphere. You would not think of ingesting a food you know to be poisonous, yet you do not realize that other's thoughts or words can be just as harmful.

Managing your personal sphere of influence involves recognizing the feedback that serves you and the feedback that doesn't. This is why you must learn to hold your own counsel.

The fewer outside opposing influences you have to reject, the less likely you will accidentally resonate with what you do not desire. The only exception to holding your counsel is when you practice the buddy system.

The buddy system involves working closely with one other person who knows your heart's desire. When you are silent about your manifestation work with everyone else you meet, you are much better able to maintain your sphere of influence.

---

[32] This was discussed at length in Chapter 3, "Boundaries and Spheres of Influence."

Your buddy supports your *Genie* work and is the only person with whom you share both your movie and your fears. The point here is to choose carefully with whom you will share manifestations so that you don't have to work overtime to reject feedback you could have avoided.

Adding emotion

There is adequate scientific proof to support this: adding emotion to your imagined outcome makes it easier to remember and feels more real. I believe that emotion is fourth-dimensional energy.

The fourth dimension is where your imagination is real and where thoughts and manifestations are not limited by time. The fabric of your reality accepts anything you feel with emotion as real. Once the reality is imbued with your emotion, the Universe sets about manifesting it for you. Research bears out that imagined outcomes can affect the reality.

> "According to the holographic model, the mind/body ultimately cannot distinguish the difference between the neural holograms the brain uses to experience reality and the ones it conjures up while imagining reality. Both have a dramatic effect on the human organism…"[33]
>
> *- This Holographic Universe* by Michael Talbot

Resonance

The EPR[34] paradox is a scientific principle that states elementary particles appear to be in communication with each other without distance or time constraints. In other words, the communication has no time lag. It is instantaneous. It's as if time is not a factor.

Ironically, the EPR Paradox has come to mean the ability for "related bits of matter, cells, even beings" to communicate **instantaneously**, without time or distance having any affect. In the original paper, Einstein et al.'s

---

[33] Talbot, Michael, *The Holographic Universe,* HarperCollins, May 1991, page 117.

[34] EPR (Einstein-Podolsky-Rosen) Paradox. Quoted in *The Holographic Universe* by Michael Talbot, page 37, it is named for the authors (Albert Einstein, Boris Podolsky and Nathan Rosen) of a widely published paper, "Can Quantum-Mechanical Description of Physical Reality be Considered Complete?" in *Physical Review*, 47 (1935), p. 777.

assertion was exactly the opposite; that faster-than-light interconnections cannot exist.

Over 25 years ago, a research paper reported an experiment where a man's saliva was sampled. It was then placed in a room separated by steel walls. Using lie detector equipment, his saliva sample was observed to produce the same reaction as the saliva in his mouth when shown various pictures including pornography. The isolated salivary fluid acted as if it never had been separated from his body.

Physicists studying subatomic particles first described this as non-locality[35] phenomenon. Though most cannot explain or believe in its reality, it has been proven to be true over and over. Particles and cells that were once linked remain linked and in resonance over distance. Time has no apparent influence. Reactions in one substance parallel reactions in the other.

100th Monkey Effect - myth or fact?

According to Wikipedia,[36] the "100th Monkey Effect" has been a popular urban myth, dating back to Lyall Watson who wrote about it in 1975 and 1979. His commentary, and later book, reports that the *hundredth monkey effect* is based on a study of macaque monkeys in Japan. Scientists observed that some monkeys learned to wash sweet potatoes, and gradually this new behavior spread through the younger generation of monkeys—in the usual fashion, through observation and repetition. Watson then claimed that the researchers observed that once a critical number of monkeys was reached—the hundredth monkey—this previously learned behavior instantly spread across the water to monkeys on a nearby island. Yet, debunkers have challenged it as a valid phenomenon.

However, current evidence can be found that seems to support it. Recently, dolphins in two different bodies of water almost simultaneously

---

[35] Nonlocality is a "buzzword" in quantum mechanics that refers to the unified whole. I would assert that this is the same as the term "void," which is found in many of the world's religions and philosophy, and from which all things come and co-exist simultaneously.

[36] Wikipedia.org, "100th Monkey Effect",
http://en.wikipedia.org/wiki/Hundredth_monkey_effect.

exhibited the ability to unhook fisherman's traps that were full of their favorite food.[37]

Resonance in physics is a principle that describes how a vibrating object can set another object vibrating harmonically with it. There are studies of pendulum clocks located in the same room that begin to swing together in unison.

Another well-documented scientific research study of resonance showed that women who worked together started to menstruate together. Amazingly this didn't occur universally. Further study led researchers to conclude that this phenomenon occurred specifically when the women had some level of cooperation and concern for one another. In other words, when they were in resonance!

Imagine driving down a dirt road where there are deep grooves from all the prior cars that have used it. You could try to drive outside of the grooves. In order to do that, you must make a significant effort. With minimal attention it is far more likely that you will find your car naturally lands in the ruts of the well-established path.

Resonance brings a vibration to its point of least resistance, which consequently uses the least amount of energy. If a room full of clocks is already moving at a certain rate, then the new arrival will move into harmony with the existing or the strongest vibration in a system.

Energy dominance

Energy dominance causes the strongest vibration in a system to dominate and homogenize the remaining elements of the system as a result of resonance. Energy dominance draws to itself more of the same.

> A thought that is a thought many times a day becomes real.
> A thought that is thought many times a day becomes more alive.
> A thought that is thought many times a day has power.
> A thought that is thought many times a day is real to the mind.
> A thought that is real to the mind is real to the Universe.

---

[37] Davis, Jingle, "Dolphins Identified as Bait Bandits," *The Atlanta Journal-Constitution,* Jan. 14, 2003.

In practical terms, energy dominance suggests that if it usually takes 20 minutes to drive to work, and you leave 10 minutes late, your arrival will be later than the 10-minute late departure. However, when you leave early, the drive will often takes less than the typical 20 minutes.

When I was a grant-writer I always finished my grants early because I hated the craziness that resulted in barely making a deadline. What I can see in hindsight is choosing to be "ahead of the wave" actually gave me a forward thrust to complete projects before their deadline.

Johnny Carson, veteran late-night talk show host, said of producing a daily TV show, "The amount of time it takes to produce a TV show is directly proportional to the amount of time between shows." How right he was!

This is true of money as well. How many businesses fail due to a lack of funding at some critical juncture? This under-funding continues to keep the business just under the edge of success, even though it may be a viable venture. I believe that everything—whether it is business or a manifestation matrix—needs a new infusion of energy to take it above its energy dominance of "not enough."

How do you overcome this? Being prepared[38] utilizes the concept of energy dominance. Make sure your energy supply—or whatever is important in the moment—is energy dominant. If your business is suffering from the early stages of poor cash flow, be prepared to take strong action, and get the funding you need before the emergency hits!

If you find yourself in this situation right now, then give at least one of your employees or all of them a raise. If you have no employees, then give your customers a freebie, or a supplier a boost. Find a way to show the Universe you are serious about moving beyond the "energy dominance" of poor cash flow.

---

[38] All of the world's wisdom literature is filled with stories and metaphors of being prepared.

Feedback

Why is resonance important? Feedback. Feedback is a mechanism of resonance. One of the early clues to the self-organizing process of resonance in nature was the discovery of a chemical reaction named after the two Soviet scientists who first described it. The Belousov-Zhabotinskii (BZ) reaction contradicts the long-held belief that chemical reactions are purely random bonding of reactant molecules. When the chemicals in the BZ reaction are put together in a shallow dish, something curious happens.

Scientists who have been looking into the chemistry of the BZ reaction now know that the order popping up from this chemical fluctuation depends on the formation of a cycle where one of the chemicals begins to produce more of itself, a *feedback* process chemists call "autocatalysis."

The *positive feedback* of autocatalysis acts like a pump creating wave fronts of active regions. Behind these fronts are quiescent regions and adjacent to them are receptive regions into which the reaction proceeds. However, within the wave fronts, the same design repeats itself on smaller and smaller scales, making the evolving pattern of the reaction fractal in nature. Can you see how nature continues to provide us with clues as to how things work?

How many of us have fond summer memories of catching fireflies in a glass jar? At first they flash randomly. Soon, however, many of them begin to flash together, and this synchronization spreads until finally the whole jarful is flashing in unison. This is another version of resonance as it operates to synchronize the flashes of fireflies in a jar. Synchronicity itself is a form of resonance.

Phase locks and feedback

Mathematicians studying the phenomenon of pulse-coupled, or phase-locked, oscillators, such as electrical oscillators, heart cells, or flashing fireflies, have learned something about how phase-locking works. As each oscillator fires, its neighbors are influenced by the *feedback* of repeated signals so that an oscillator close to its firing threshold senses a signal from its neighbor and fires off immediately. At that point oscillators become locked together. Scientists think this process proceeds until all of the oscillators—whether fireflies or heartbeats—become coupled.

It is this principle of feedback that demonstrates the direct relationship between the Phoenix Sequence and any manifestation. Remember, in nonlinear systems, negative feedback keeps a system in place, and positive feedback allows a system to move and make dramatic changes.[39] Negative thoughts maintain the status quo. Positive thoughts create dramatic changes that may not be visible immediately, but are eventually realized.

Nigel Reading, writer on chaos theory states: "Life-forms, ecosystems, global climate, plate tectonics, celestial mechanics, human economies, history and societies, even consciousness itself—all manifest this feedback-led, reflexive behavior; they maximize their adaptive capacities by entering this region of (maximum) complexity on the edge of Chaos, whenever they are pushed far from their equilibrium states, thereby incrementally increasing their internal complexity, between occasional 'catastrophes.' Remarkably, this transition zone is mathematically occupied by the Golden Mean."[40] Bear in mind, any Phoenix Sequence produces Phi, also known as the Golden Mean, regardless of its origins.

Remember how chaos theory explains that feedback is the source of the complexity found in chaos? Understanding chaos theory allowed me to recognize that *feedback* was the major factor in getting the outcome I wanted. Just like an artist, I could control many of the factors—including the feedback—going onto the canvas of my life in order to obtain a certain kind of result. I realized that I was free to accept or reject feedback.

If I accepted feedback from someone telling me something wasn't possible, it could affect my outcome. If I refused to believe feedback that didn't serve my heart's desire, or me, then I could control enough of the factors to get my preferred result. This was something I had known intuitively for years, but now I had found a scientific explanation that could be used by anyone who needed a more logical approach to manifestation.

---

[39] Chaos is "really a highly complex form of hierarchical, enfolded order that appears to be disorder... As mentioned, iterated recursive loops [feedback] must occur over a certain time interval and have a beginning and an end." From Reading, Nigel, "Dynamical Symmetries: Autopoietic Architecture" at:
http://reocities.com/Area51/starship/9201/phimega/phimega.html.
[40] Ibid.

Think about all the things you allow into your personal sphere. You have favorite music, books, TV shows and movies. While they are generally used for entertainment, it is possible to use these media purposefully to enhance your *Genie* work.

Deliberately watch movies that run a version of your own personal movie, or listen to songs that carry the message of your heart's desire. While you are manifesting the partner of your dreams, it is far better to have a love song of inspiration than of unrequited love playing endlessly in your head. While these songs have their place in the reality, excessive use of sad songs especially, contribute to the general feeling of the impossibility of satisfying love.

In Chapter 9 there is a discussion of using music and recordings as tools. When you are on a diet you have a specific, focused outcome in mind, and you avoid things that are not on your diet. Likewise, when working on manifesting a life filled with your heart's desires, it may serve you to avoid certain influences that do not support it.

Summary

Resistance is about how you change. When bad things happen it is your duty to yourself to look for some benefit from this bad thing. If you resist too much you may discover that you will bring more of the thing you are resisting. Paying attention to what you are resisting will help you understand it.

There are four kinds of resistance. Each kind has something to show you. The first kind is expressed as envy, and is rooted in a fear that there isn't enough. The second kind of resistance is based more on stubbornness, and is a result of wanting things to be different, without being willing to *do* anything different.

The third level of resistance is usually based on some childhood experience that caused you to think "this is the way the world operates." It generally isn't true, but it takes a little more awareness to recognize it. Asking for help from the angelic realm or a licensed professional is particularly helpful at this level.

The fourth level of resistance is denial. When the same things keep happening, it is important to look at why you don't seem to be "getting it." Then the information tends to come forth. When you are certain it's not you and yet the same thing keeps coming back, be willing to look at it and see the solution opening up.

Learning to recognize your resistance and finding ways to shift and change will help you reclaim your power. Your resistance sometimes is a helpful tool to hone your persistence skills.

Remember that you can learn optimistic behaviors. You can search out and find reasons to see a benefit in everything that happens. You can examine all the possible causes behind a disappointing situation and see what benefit you can take from it. Looking for and finding real tangible evidence takes you beyond the Pollyanna stage of positive thinking to scientific proof that allows you to shift your focus and benefit from new knowledge of your thought process.

Everyone has a contract with the Universe. Exercise your options. Look at what is incoming and use what is put in front of you. You may discover options you didn't know you had. Mohammed Ali learned to box in order to catch and beat a thief, and boxing became his lifelong passion. Your upset can lead to new interests just like him.

If you believe the Universe has unlimited possibilities, it must mean there are multiple solutions to every problem. Be flexible and open to other solutions. Anything with which you resonate will serve as a magnet to bring in more of the same. Become aware of all the influences you allow into your inner sphere including music, books, TV and movies. Since this feedback can become a resonator limit it by selecting only the things you choose to resonate with.

Energy dominance in a system leads to more of the same kind of energy. Use this principle to your advantage. Resonance will occur wherever there is an abundance of similar energy; then the dominance of that energy is a foregone conclusion. Focus your attention on what you desire to increase and it will grow.

Let energy dominance work for you, not against you. Being a little late will result in being a lot late. Focus on what is working. Use the principle of energy dominance to your advantage.

Chapter 9

Tools

I had just facilitated a very successful dolphin swim and workshop in Hawaii. A day before the workshop ended, I had received a phone call at 4 AM from my younger brother. He gave me the terrible news that our sister, his twin, had been killed in an automobile accident in France, where she had made her home with her husband and children. Everyone was devastated. Because of this event, I immediately headed for France, leaving Hawaii early.

One of the men in my workshop, Michael, decided to travel to the airport with me since he was catching a later flight that day. Although he needed a ride, his motivation in returning early was to support me, as I was consumed in grief.

We arrived at the airport with very little extra time. I was starting to feel stressed because I had to return the rental car and go through security and time was tight. We drove around the circle of the little airport three times without finding the location to return the rental car.

I wanted to scream in frustration, but what could I say to express my frustration that would be in keeping with who I really am? So I said in a very frustrated way, "Well, the angels are going to have to show me how *really good* they are."

We finally stopped a guard on our third time around the airport circle and he told us that we had to exit the airport circle to get to the car rental return. No one had told us the rental return had been moved, and was now situated *outside* of the airport!

As we pulled into the rental drop-off lot, Michael offered to be the porter for both of us. I carried my tote bag and Michael took responsibility for everything else.

After an inventory of our possessions, I pointed to the large liter-sized bottle of water that was half full and said, "Michael, if you have to, you can leave the water behind. We can always get more water in the airport."

Of course, I was selected for extra security screening. While we were waiting for the security-scanned luggage, I finally started to relax a little and realized how thirsty I was. I asked, "Michael, did you bring the water?" He was lost in thought and didn't seem to hear me. I looked at my open tote bag and there was the half-full liter of water. I was so relieved; I just started drinking from it.

Just then, Michael turned to me, seemed surprised and said, "Maureen, did you bring the water?" "No." I responded. "Well, I didn't either. I left it in the rental car. It was the last thing I saw when I closed the car door."

It was at that moment that I knew the rest of the trip would be fine, even though I was traveling to Paris without my passport in hand, relying on others to get it to me en route. I knew the angels were hard at work.

There are several tools in the *Genie System*:

1. Ask for Help – from Angels and a Higher Power
2. Learn the Art of Two-fers – follow every negative thought with two positive thoughts
3. Write it Down – make lists: to do lists, wish lists, desire lists
4. Make your own Recordings – and learn how to use them
5. Put Events on your Calendar – keep your schedule visible
6. Maureen's Manifestation Matrix – for overcoming obstacles
7. Pre-pay for Events you Wish to Attend – when the time comes, money won't be an issue
8. Recycle Fear – which you already know about from Chapter 6
9. Look for Synchronicity – to provide support when the Divinity Tests come
10. Ask for Benevolent Outcomes – also detailed in Chapter 6
11. Ask for a Day of Heaven on Earth! – state your intention to the Universe

Ask for help

Sometimes you may not be able to get past your fears and worries. Calling for help from the Angels or a Higher Power is powerful and effective. It doesn't mean you aren't going to do your work. It means you are getting a little help from a source that knows more than you do. Over and over, the individuals I work with continue to provide me with feedback that tells me when they ask for help in their prayer work that everything shifts. What have you got to lose?

If you were a golfer, and had a regular weekly game, would you consider it an unfair advantage if someone introduced you to Tiger Woods, and arranged private lessons from him? Similarly, calling Angels or another Higher Power may be the just the help you need. The price is right, and they are experts who are eager to assist you.

Learn the art of two-fers

The *Genie System* allows negative thoughts. Most manifestation books will tell you that you must limit your negative thinking. While that may be helpful, you may need to express your frustration or disappointments when they occur.

Sometimes your negative thoughts seem to come out of nowhere. Sometimes you are so "down" you don't want to monitor your thoughts. Simply make sure each negative thought is followed with two comparable thoughts of a positive nature, *two-fers*.

Two-fers allow you to express negative thoughts as frequently as you wish, because you are always required to follow them with two positive ones. The first positive always neutralizes the negative thought, the second is your *seed*. Put your attention on the two-fers and have some fun with it.

Doing two-fers is not sandwiching the negative thoughts between the two positives ones. It is finding two positives that are as real and tangible as the negative thought is to you. This is because the negative thoughts come in randomly and you cannot know or anticipate their presence. It is only after you have had a negative thought that you can catch yourself thinking that thought and then do something about it. Follow it with two positive thoughts of related value.

When I was in college my parents convinced me to transfer to a different college. I had lots of reasons why I didn't like this new college. One of the reasons I didn't like it was that it was an all-women's school, and there were no men around. I remember feeling so unhappy about where I was. Finally, in my prayer work, I asked for some help from my angels.

I believe the help I received was the idea to practice two-fers. For example, if I hated this school because there were no boys there, then I had to have two reasons why the school was a good one without guys.

My two-fers looked like this: I could roll out of bed and go to class without fixing my hair or dressing up; and I could study intensely during the week without distractions and then party all weekend—guilt free. I found myself naturally sharing my two positive thoughts whenever any of my new friends at college would complain about our school or dorm life.

I was getting so proficient at offering the positive attributes of my new college that the Director of Admissions heard about me. I had been at the school only six weeks when she asked me to lead guided tours to prospective students! My mother's reaction was classic, "Talk about the blind leading the blind."

Write it down

Start by writing down a list of everything you want to accomplish in life. Place it in a book or file to be located later. My current list has over 300 things on it. Then think about what you would like to accomplish this year, write it down and put it away.

Make a list of things you'd like to get to this month. Set that aside. Make a list of things you want to get done this week. You won't even have to look at that again! Research has shown that 90% of individuals who make "to do lists" never look at them again – yet manage to get most, if not all, on their list accomplished. How is this possible? Just the act of writing, capturing a thought onto paper, shows the Universe you are serious about it, and events and activities form around them – almost effortlessly.

When my children were little I was superintendent of Sunday school. I guess they put me in charge because I brought so many kids to the church!

I gave out the lessons for each of the teachers and asked them, "Please read this tonight, Sunday night."

If they did that, during the week, without fail, the teachers would discover helpful ideas, crafts and tools to present the lessons. They were always telling me how excited they were about the great ideas that they got during the week! I believe this was because by reading the lesson, the teacher was making a clear intent to the Universe, "I intend to teach this class – and I'm looking for ideas."

Make your own recordings

One of the more advanced tools you can use is to record your voice on your phone or other audio device stating your "movie of the mind" and play it back to yourself. Much like a nostalgic, one-actor play, hearing it spoken by you in the past tense can really give you a jump-start on your manifestation movies.

It may be easier for you to relax into your pleasurable feelings when you listen to your recorded *Genie* Movie. It also helps you gain perspective of your movie to make sure all the elements are being met. Have fun, play with it!

You may find that you desire to play your recording often. I recommend you play it no more than three times in a day. At some point you will forget about it and that is OK too. It means that the movie is forming its own reality and doesn't need you to continue to replay your movie of the mind to insure the outcome.

Put events on your calendar

One year, after attending the annual convention of my trade association, I decided I really wanted to attend next year's convention. Shortly after that, my job ended, putting into question the likelihood of attending.

I put it on my calendar for next year (the meeting was still 11 months in the future). I almost forgot about it, because I had been looking for another full-time job for so long. I still wanted to go to the annual meeting, even though unemployed.

My new job began just one week before the annual meeting, and it wasn't the exact same industry. At my third interview I approached my potential employer about attending. She reminded me that it wasn't the same industry. I agreed, but showed her that there were some cross-over classes that could be useful.

She said there was no money in the budget for such a trip, but then paused, asking what city it was in? It turned out that there was an unused ticket purchased for that very city that was going to expire in three weeks! She would check to see if I could fly under someone else's name.

This was long before flying on someone else's ticket wasn't possible. Then she mused, "We still don't have money for your tuition." I countered that sometimes the association has scholarships. I could investigate that. "Yes, but what about accommodations?" I responded, "I have lots of friends in that city, I can probably stay with someone there!"

I called the national association. When I asked the staff member about a scholarship for the convention (just 10 days away at this point), she credulously asked, "For this year?" "Yes." I replied with great enthusiasm in my voice, telling her that I had airfare and accommodations covered. "Oh, all of our scholarships for this year were given away eight months ago."

I waited politely. Then she asked, "How long have you been attending?" "Nine years." She continued, "And this is the first year you haven't been able to attend due to budget constraints?" "Yes," I replied, again with enthusiasm. Her voice brightened, "I think I can find one more scholarship for you."

In my seminar business, I tell everyone who has barriers to attending my workshops to "Put the workshop on your calendar!" Then tell the Universe you wish to attend, and name your barriers. The barriers could be availability issues, money constraints, time off from work, childcare obligations or the like. Then state, "If the barriers are taken care of – I'll do my part, and show up!"

Maureen's Manifestation Matrix

Over the years I have developed a very easy-to-use tool called "Maureen's Manifestation Matrix" for people who wish to attend my workshops. This tool will help you clear all your obstacles to attending any event. We have had great results over the years. I invite you to use my manifestation matrix that incorporates these tools. It is printed below, and can also be found on my website.[41] It reads as follows:

This is for anyone who wishes to take classes with Maureen or any teacher! You may benefit from Maureen's Manifestation Matrix by naming and requesting it. If it is truly your desire to attend this workshop and you are serious about it, then do the following:

1. Take your request to the altar. If you don't have an altar, you might want to make an altar for yourself. Your altar is a sacred place that contains items you find sacred and is a place where you might meditate. The altar of your heart is also acceptable.
2. State clearly what your desire/intention is (to attend Maureen's workshop, etc.) and what constraints you may have, such as time off from work, dollars, family obligations or responsibilities, etc. and agree to do your part (i.e. show up) and then let the Universe work its magic for you.
3. You will do your part if the Universe does its part. Then mark your personal calendar with the class dates, tell everyone you intend to be there and that you are expecting a miracle (NOT HOPING for but EXPECTING A MIRACLE).
4. Then SEE yourself at the class. Relax into it, knowing you are already there and then let go. Let yourself feel your gratitude for fulfilling your heart's desire. You are a beloved being and deserve to have your heart's desire.

And, from one of our clients…

I've tried the manifestation matrix, and it worked. It brought something really precious to me. :) - Zoltan

---

[41] MaureenStGermain.com, "Manifestation Matrix",
http://www.maureenstgermain.com/Tools.html#Manifest.

Pre-pay for events you wish to attend

Pre-paying for an event is one of the powerful ways you can support your intention of attending it. Money is energy. When you put your money into an event, energy forms around the event and it starts to coalesce around the event and make it real.

In April, when Donna Brown meditated on her next trip to Egypt in October, she saw herself at Abu Simbel with a group of people. Donna had traveled to Egypt with me before and some of the same people returned with us. However, in her meditation, she saw two people she had never met—all the others were "faceless people."

After our group experienced Abu Simbel we had our usual wrap-up session to discuss our experiences. Donna shared that the two people who were in her meditation last April were two new people who were on our trip, one a very distinctive looking Native American woman named Ann, and another distinctly French woman Marie-Claude. How is it that these two unmistakable individuals, whom Donna never met, could have shown up in her earlier meditation?

Both women had paid in full for the October trip in mid-March. Apparently, the quantum field was already forming around this event as they were putting their money into it. They effectively "seeded" the future event with their energy, making it possible for Donna to experience them in her meditation about a future event.

In the seminar business, I have found that when individuals start registering for a workshop – it invariably creates a vortex that draws more people in. For the Egypt trip, those three individuals with their strong commitment to participate created enough of a matrix to materialize the events that actually occurred.

Donna's tuning in to the event, experienced as a future event in her meditation, included those individuals who had committed their energy to that project. If you really want an event to take place, don't wait around for the last minute to sign up. Let your payment send a strong signal to the Universe that you are serious about attending.

Recycle fear

This is mentioned again here as a tool because of its importance. The full discussion is found in Chapter 6. Your fear can be recycled to help you move forward in your manifestations. Use your fear to fuel your manifestation by recycling it and using it to fund your manifestation movie.

When optimism is down – do something to jump-start your system – give employees a raise, decide to push into the wind and use it to your advantage. Remember the phrase, "When the going gets tough, the tough get going." An engineer in Chicago, Eugene Maurey,[42] who owned a manufacturing facility, always practiced this rule of giving company-wide raises when sales were down. It effectively boosted morale and resulted in increased sales. You can find ways to do that for yourself!

Look for synchronicity

If you remember the movie Man of La Mancha – the protagonist dared to dream the impossible dream. He also chased windmills. How do you know if the dream you are chasing is a windmill? You let go. Once you release your attachment to having your outcome, in your time frame, you will experience synchronicities that point the way.

Synchronicity is hearing a song in your head whose words reinforce a difficult decision but tells you to keep the faith. It could be getting an unexpected telephone call of support for a project or idea you "let go." It could be meeting just the right person who will help make your dreams real. Look for those synchronicities to help you know that the rainbow you are chasing is real and attainable.

Ask for benevolent outcomes

Recently I have come across information that invites you to ask for a benevolent outcome,[43] especially when incoming data presents information that is radically different from your stated goals and desires. When you begin any project, ask for "a most benevolent outcome."

---

[42] Maurey, Eugene, *Power of Thought*, pages 55-56
[43] Moore, Tom, *The Gentle Way*

I was working with a second run of my first CD, which had sold out within the first six months. I had put a lot of work into the writing, recording, and mixing of this meditation. I was thrilled with the original cover art developed by the art department of the pressing company.

The rerun arrived and I discovered the cover printing was inferior. The company offered a $200 rebate on my next order. I was outraged by their meager offer. Yet I understood that they didn't see the problem as I did. My CD was very special to me, and I wanted the cover to be perfect.

It took a while for me to realize any size rebate from them would be unsatisfactory. What I really desired was a redo of the cover with the colors exactly matched to the initial run. I understood this was a tall order, and through a series of events, all within 20 minutes of the phone call, they finally agreed to do just that. I never had to yell or scream, or cry or whine. All I did was ask for a most benevolent outcome before I picked up the phone.

Ask for a Day of Heaven on Earth!

I was just returning to Wisconsin on a flight from Seattle when I ran into a familiar face, one of the United Airlines employees who greeted me by name. "How are you doing today, Maureen?" was her cheery greeting. I had been flying all night and was concerned about my schedule that required me to get on another plane in about 5 hours. I responded, "Pretty good, but this is my day from h*ll, because I have to be back here in 3 hours to get on a plane to the East coast." She looked at me, not sure what to say, and before she could respond I quickly added, "Actually this is a *Day of Heaven on Earth* because I am flying with United!" She smiled and nodded and we both went about our business.

I had realized, as soon as those words came out of my mouth, that I didn't want to be perceived this way (by the agent or the Universe), which is why I made the verbal correction. United Airlines has always taken good care of me.

Upon arriving home, I discovered a flood in my basement. A water pipe had sprung a leak somewhere between the walls the day before. My roommate had heard the running water, and knew about it, but chose to ignore it since she couldn't locate it.

I quickly shut off the water and called one of my neighbors, Gene. Fortunately he was home, and came over to look into it. We called the plumber who said he would be there in an hour. While waiting for the plumber, I called the airline asking if they could book me on a later flight that same day, which they confirmed. Gene came back to my house to supervise the plumber and insisted that I go about my necessary chores, taking care of my office needs and re-packing my suitcase.

I had a number of things that had to get done since I only had a few hours to get the next flight. The plumber was on time, fixed the problem, and I got all my errands done. I realized that I was really close to making my original flight. I mused, "I really only needed an extra half hour and I could have made my flight." Then the electronic voice mail announcements from United to my cell phone came in to announce their flights were running late today.

Just then the phone rang; it was a local United Airlines agent who had called to tell me that she didn't think I would make my connections on the later flight I was reserved for. Would it be possible for me to make the earlier flight (the one I was originally booked on), but now was departing an hour later? I was packed and ready, and able to leave the house within 15 minutes. I caught the flight.

That's when I realized how powerful my new statement, "I am having a Day of Heaven on Earth," really is. I have experienced numerous experiments with this statement and I now recommend you use it daily! Why not?

I also suggest that before getting out of bed each morning that you state your intention to the Universe. Part of my daily mantra has been, "I always choose to feel good! Nothing is more important. No matter where I am, no matter what I am doing, no matter who I am with - I choose to see the positive aspects in everyone and everything. I am satisfied with where I am and eager for more. I always make the best of wherever I am."

One very important aspect in finding your way to feeling good is to be okay with where you are, knowing that as you make the best of it, things

143

just have to get better and better. It's the Law of Attraction in action - what you focus on expands! And now I always finish with, "I am asking for a Day of Heaven on Earth this day."

Summary – The *Genie* Tools

Ask the Angels or your Higher Power for help in fulfilling your heart's desire. All of heaven is waiting for you to ask for their help. Do this at least once a day. This is because each day is a new beginning. Each day is a day to practice free will and claim your Divine Inheritance.

Practice the art of two-fers. Resisting negative thoughts may increase them. Instead, allow the entire negative thought to have a voice and then follow with two-fers. Remember, your positive two-fers must be at parity with the negative thought. Commit your desires, ideas, lists to paper. Just the act of writing shows the Universe you are serious about it, and events and activities will form around them almost effortlessly.

Make an audio recording of your movie and play it up to three times a day. When you forget about it, this means the movie is forming its own reality.

Put events you plan or want to attend on the calendar, even if it appears unlikely you can attend. If your intention is clear, the Universe will help find a way for you to be there.

Maureen's Manifestation Matrix is a tool you can use to help clear all your obstacles. EXPECT a miracle!

You should pre-pay for events. The Universe respects your intention when you "put your money where your mouth is."

When fear overtakes you, remember to recycle!

Use synchronicity to help you distinguish between the "impossible" dream and the fantastic.

Remember to ask for a most benevolent outcome. This shifts and adjusts everything you are working on to the most beneficial outcome for all involved. This creates a win-win situation everywhere you go, and with everyone you encounter.

Finally, ask for a Day of Heaven on Earth. Then watch the magic happen!

Chapter 10

Putting It All Together

In the previous chapters, you have learned about "The Practices" of creating your *Genie* Manifestation. In the following section, "The Principles & Proofs," you will discover the importance of understanding the basic laws of creation from a scientific perspective. You will learn that conscious knowledge of this information will allow you to become a conscious creator. This will dispel any doubt and move you beyond your wildest expectations.

What does quantum physics tell you about the nature of reality? It teaches that more than one version of an outcome exists, until a particular version is observed. When you combine sacred geometry with quantum physics, you now have a new way to understand creation in the reality and can apply these principles to manifest what you desire.

All possibilities exist. You are choosing one. You are maintaining your own personal sphere; yet, you agree to the conditions of the Mass Consciousness Sphere more often than you realize. This means you must selectively choose what you wish to manifest and leave all the other details to mass consciousness. Mass consciousness has been on autopilot for a long time, and it is perfectly OK to live with it while you gain your mastery.

Everything you think of can be manifested. Your ability to manifest is as unlimited as the quantum soup is infinite. All possibilities exist. All opportunities already exist. All you are doing is going into the void of all possibilities and selecting the possibility that exists in your mind's eye. This selection can now be pulled from the void because it resonates with your thought. The emotion in your thought will cause it to resonate with and magnetize to you.

You will learn about the two kinds of creation, linear and spiral. You'll begin to understand that the mathematical laws show us everything contains the Phi ratio, and that using Phi will produce for you everything that you require to attain your outcome. Your job is to maintain the integrity of the system of manifestation.

The way you do that is through limiting the feedback and applying the law of resonance (found in Chapter 8). The *Genie System* guarantees that all you have to do is be clear in your intent, limit your spheres of influence, stay in integrity, and then let go!

You have made use of steps in creating your heart's desire in order to maximize your efforts and stay on target. You need to be aware of all your thoughts and desires, and know which ones may be standing in your way. There is a fine line between *naming* your fears and *avoiding* them.

Using fear to fuel the *Genie*

You have learned that it is crucial to *hear* the positive intent of your fear message, but it is not required to *heed* it! This is especially true if the message is some form of "You will fail" message. Your job is to learn to discern fear messages by their source, that is, to determine if they are coming from your inner sphere or if they are coming from the outer spheres.

Once you know the source of your fear you can act. If your fear is coming from inside you, and it is showing you your actions and desires don't match up, you will choose to alter your behavior or change your belief system.

If you discover that the messages are coming from one of the external spheres you can choose to ignore messages that do not serve you by simply dismissing them. You have begun to understand that you cannot avoid incoming messages, but that once heard, you *can* disregard them.

Once you bless the messenger for doing what he believes is his job, he can quit bothering you! In this way you have effectively maintained your sphere of influence.

You have learned to limit feedback in another way, by limiting the individuals you share your personal movies with. Keep your *Genie* work to yourself. You will find that working with one or two trusted friends or advisors will be all that you need to keep you on course and keep your manifestations blooming!

The matrix of our Universe is living and breathing. Your matrix probably has been on autopilot for a long time and everything happened according to very definable laws. Just by reading this, you are now coming of age, and beginning to understand that *you can be in the matrix but not ruled by it;* that you can have your own version of the matrix controlled by your personal sphere.

Maintaining integrity

Maintaining your personal integrity is the single most powerful tool you have to support your creations. Once you understand that the Universe takes you quite literally, you no longer need to act outside of integrity. This was discussed fully in Chapter 3, "Boundaries and Spheres of Influence."

Some individuals have lots of integrity, others less. It is important to note that as you upgrade your equipment, you will discover that your "new equipment" won't function with some of the old energies you used to work with. You may discover that you need to act differently. A way to test your integrity is to read Brad Blanton's book, "Radical Honesty".[44] This book will help you notice where your integrity needs a boost.

It may also mean that when you start to change, some of your friends won't make it into your new matrix if they don't upgrade too. Nothing can stop you if you deal with your fear/negativity/pain and are willing to increase your population of positive thoughts to bring in your outcome. Do not waste any time on self-recrimination. Ten years from now, will it make any difference?

Remember to find the positives that go with a change. To illustrate, following a job loss, you may have dipped into your savings that you planned to use for a new home. Now you have less money or no money for the down payment. Perhaps though, you will discover that your partner

---

[44] Blanton, Brad, "Radical Honesty", Sparrowhawk Publications; Revised edition (March 29, 2005).

can now take a promotion to another city and you are much more available to move, due to the unexpected job loss.

Many have stumbled on these principles or applied them accidentally. Many have experienced parts of these principles without seeing the total picture. The more strongly you allow yourself permission to be unique, and to be a fully actualized human, the more you will begin to realize how easy it is for you to manifest the reality you wish for yourself.

You are the CEO of your own personal corporation. The Universe provides the materials and employees. Your job is to navigate and direct. **Your job is to focus on *what* you want, not *how* to get it.** The "how it will occur" will be shown to you.

Creating your heart's desire

You will not work backwards, but simply leap into an already existing future with your movie. Your "heart's desire" comes as a natural occurrence based on cause and effect. Your quantum creation at the "outcome" level, or the "effect" level, causes certain things to happen at the creation level. And like a mathematical equation, you can then know with absolute certainty that the circumstances you need to cause your desired outcome will occur.

Creating your *Genie* Movie

In the next section, *The Principles & Proofs*, you will learn the details of making *Genie* Movies and why they always work.

Once you have created the movie of your heart's desire, the known forces of the Universe will force your creation to occur. All you have to do is show up! Showing up means you are willing to do the work that is put before you. Landing an interview doesn't get the job. However, it does give you the *opportunity* to be hired!

Your movie-of-the-mind

Start from a place where your movie reflects the fact that your heart's desire has already existed in your reality. In your movie, you will always be looking at your outcome as if it is a *past event*. This is important. If

149

your heart's desire is a happy marriage, you don't see your wedding. Instead, you see yourself being happily married to your beloved at some significant time after your marriage, proving that you are already together, joyfully celebrating an anniversary at a lovely dinner, clinking glasses as you beam at each other, sharing how happy you are, including the actual words each of you say.

Learn to "suspend disbelief"

When you go to the movie theater, you "suspend disbelief" to enjoy the movie. By suspending disbelief in your personal "movie," you begin to experience the true emotions of enjoying the effects of your desired outcome. This will be really fun! This can give you great pleasure!

For the newly desired outcome you can use your *present* to define your current problems and needs. As you look at what you desire in life, you create your new *present* situation. You selectively choose what you are willing to accept from your job, co-workers, family and friends and discard everything else.

Selective hearing isn't healthy in relationships; but useful in your *Genie* work. Your ability to discriminate between what you accept and reject is crucial to creating your desired outcome. You may find that this helps you get clarity on what you truly desire.

You have learned that recycling means you clear your fear of its negative charge and use the clean energy to fund your lighthouse. Funding is a powerful word that implies full support. Fund your lighthouse with positive emotion.

Look for synchronicities

When doubt moves in, look for synchronicities that reinforce your direction. If your manifestation is about moving to and living in Chicago, and you start meeting people from Chicago, the Universe is showing you your *Genie* Movie outcome is moving towards you.

These synchronicities occur to give you the added boost that you will need to see your way through the Divinity Tests that may come along. The synchronicities show you that you are on the right track, help you "keep the faith" and stay the course towards your heart's desire.

As you manifest, you create circumstances that cause you to open your heart more. You find it much easier to be generous because you no longer feel that there is not enough. This changes your attitude towards strangers as well as yourself. And it is your opportunity to gain mastery on all fronts.

When you fall down – get back up quickly

Along the way you have chances to falter, and to gain an in-depth awareness of your fears and foibles. When fear comes up, use your tools to help you move through it (Chapter 9). You have learned to practice two-fers, to work with a trusted individual to reinforce your dream, and to make that leap of faith.

Don't worry about whether you will fall down; concern yourself with how quickly you can recover! When circumstances appear to rob you of your outcome, hold your heart's desire clearly and firmly. It's important to remember that there will be many divinity moments. If you know you will have Divinity Tests, you can prepare for them. How do you prepare?

Fear is a messenger

Remember that fear is a messenger. Many individuals have succeeded at a fire walk, but no one can do it for you! When you do have fear, remember that fear is a messenger, and that once you have heard the message, you still have that raw energy you can use to fund your outcome. Send that energy to your lighthouse, and run your movie!

You don't have to do anything more than hold your belief system so strongly that you will not let anything interfere in your creation. If you waver too much you may need to take smaller steps. Smaller steps keep you from manifesting something that is bigger than what you believe in, which you could not maintain.

Your Divinity Test

The Divinity Test is about you believing in yourself. My friend, Teresa, was a very successful Canadian stock trader and adviser living in Alberta, Canada. She made a six-figure income. She was also dating an American from Seattle. Suddenly her job was being eliminated. Her company gave her six months' notice, was paying severance and providing outplacement counseling.

The outplacement evaluations showed that she would be good as a technical writer. She took advantage of all the training she could get to open doors into a new career. She was offered another job in her old field that would require a lot of travel throughout Canada and make her new love interest relationship impossible. She said no to the job and her boyfriend proposed.

Her new home, in her husband's town, Seattle, was an ideal location for her new career path. She looked for work in both her old and new profession. After accepting a few small contract jobs in her new profession, a "dream" job opened in her old profession where she would be earning double what she was earning in her new profession. Her husband wanted her to take it. Teresa wasn't sure.

What's a Divinity Test like?

The Divinity Test asks you, "Are you serious about your new profession?" Yes! Teresa took the lower paying job to grow and advance her new career. She was willing to take the risk on herself and invest in her future. Are you serious about yours?

Let yourself gain experience and let it continue to provide opportunities for you to extend your mastery. So start small and work your way up. Baseball teams in the States have "farm teams" to give their prospects the chance to get experience and confidence in their abilities before they play in the major leagues. Sports teams the world over practice as much as a week for each game. So consider your practice an important part of developing your manifestation skills.

Don't worry about time. I believe our sciences are on the verge of understanding time in a new way. Time is really a convention that allows you to examine parts of life more closely. Use time to give yourself a clean slate, and to let go of the past. The past is not necessarily an indicator of the future. It is a way to look at the experiences of the reality and chose differently the next time.

Learn to "allow" two versions of the reality

Remember that the reality may look like one thing, but you are choosing your own outcome. If all conditions look like you will not get your outcome, don't go into grief! Choose to back up, go to the fork in the road, and let the Universe show you another way to let your dream come true.

Your job is to make a movie showing that your desired outcome has already come true. Your movie addresses your outcome event, but begins after it has occurred. Your movie is always a reflection of what has occurred, and how your life is significantly different now that it has happened. Looking back at the past from a new present moment can be illustrated in the following manner.

If you wanted to have a wonderful wedding, your movie might look like this:

> *You are sitting in the arms of your beloved, a number of years after the wedding, and reflecting on what a nice wedding reception it was.*

If your focus is on finding your divine partner, your movie might begin in the same way, but you would be reflecting on how happy you are as a couple, how magical your courtship was, etc. Your movie always is experienced in a "present tense," while looking at the past outcome.

From the time perspective of reading this book, all the events are in the future.

The one detail your manifestation does not include is *how* it occurred. If you find yourself expressing thoughts about *how* your dream will come true, then you are in your logical brain. Although this may be useful in planning a strategy, it does not belong in your manifestation movie.

Others have free will too

Remember that you do have control over what thoughts get to live in your head. There are many experiences that you have in your life where your parents or other significant caregivers taught you that things have to happen a certain way.

They also taught you how to accept and reject advice. All you have to remember is to evaluate the feedback as beneficial or not. If it is not beneficial, then simply reject it. The law of resonance shows you that what you think about is what you will attract. So don't spend a whole lot of energy on expressing your feelings about what you don't want. If you do, the Universe will give you more of your "don't wants."

If you cannot seem to get "what you don't want" out of your head, because, let's presume, you are so darned angry about something, then make a list of what you don't want and create a second list from the first that re-frames your "don't want" list into a desire list.

Summary

In the *Genie System*, manifesting your heart's desire is based on understanding sacred geometry (Chapter 13), understanding yourself and finding ways to experience the reality in a new way. It invites you to shift and adjust as necessary.

Stay in balance, and use both sides of your brain. Use your logic to take you through various steps that you know you need to do, and use your intuitive side to capture, act on, and be responsive to the spontaneous opportunities that will surely come your way.

Add your emotion, the feeling of having your heart's desire. Focus your feelings on the event AFTER the heart's desired event occurs. By focusing on the event *after* you have achieved your heart's desire, you will provide the two focal points that continue to serve as the anchors to bring your manifestation into reality.

The two focal points – today and after events – serve to focus your attention on your heart's desire. They serve to take you into the quantum zone of all possibilities, and they hold you there because each provides a reference point for the other. You satisfy your conscious mind by capitalizing on the known aspects of your reality by using your understanding of linear equations and quantum physics (Chapter 16).

You control the feedback, selecting what serves your heart's desire and rejecting all else. The two focal points provide the two numbers in your Phoenix Sequence, which allows magic to happen (Chapter 14). This is a mathematical formula that forces your heart's desire to occur. When you add your emotion, you give your manifestation a jump-start.

One of the most effective ways to boost your manifestation power is to continue to do your spiritual work. Take classes. Keep evolving and learning. Let everyone you meet teach you something. See the wonder and joy of the Universe.

In your heart of hearts you may long to be non-judgmental. It is your nature to be open and accepting. Yet, you may have discovered that in real life you have been dealt some unjust and unfair circumstances. You may have anger and bitterness about lots of things.

As you learn to manifest you will choose to let those judgments go. You will see that those feelings keep giving you more of what you don't want. Choose to resonate what you desire, so that the Universe brings you more of it.

If you can learn to be more loving towards yourself, and open your heart, you will go a long way towards manifesting your heart's desire. There are many ways to learn how to do this. I highly recommend the MerKaBa meditation.[45] In my opinion, learning the MerKaBa meditation and how to connect with your Higher Self will do more to enhance your ability to amplify the *Genie* work than any other spiritual practice.

---

[45] MaureenStGermain.com, *MerKaBa Classic* meditation workshop, http://www.maureenstgermain.com/FlowerofLifeWorkshop.html.

I highly recommend that you discover for yourself what helps you keep your heart open. There are lots of books, seminars and prayers that will assist you.[46] This book cannot teach you everything about getting in touch with your feelings and connecting with your heart. Find the practice that works for you, and with patience, you will gain that mastery. Any heart opening experience will aid your *Genie* work.

Learn to live life in your heart. Fall more in love with life than you ever have been before. Let go of judgments of situations that you have perceived as bad, unjust, or unfair. You will be thankful for the opportunities the experiences gave you to change, to see life differently, to love yourself, and to love life.

May you discover that you really *can* "Be a Genie!" I wish you a most benevolent outcome on your journey.

---

[46] Recommended Books: *Beyond the Flower of Life* by Maureen St. Germain, *Living in the Heart* by Drunvalo Melchizedek. Video: *MerKaBa Classic* DVD by Maureen St. Germain. Audio: *Connecting with your Higher Self* audio course by Maureen St. Germain.

Part II

The Principles & Proofs

Chapter 11

What's It All About?

My very first out-of-state workshop set the standard. I had convinced my dear friend, Winona, to host my workshop. She told me "Maureen, you know I love you, and would love any workshop you would do, but I live in an area that isn't really open to this sort of thing." My response was always optimistic. I took inspiration from the movie, *Field of Dreams*, and insisted that if she would agree to host it, the people would come!

That wasn't the only obstacle. She had a very tiny house, and three small children. She was worried about how we would squeeze a workshop into this space and still have her children running around. I was undaunted.

The day before the workshop, Winona's best friend's mother called. She was a real estate agent in this little resort town, and had heard about Winona hosting the workshop from her daughter. She said to her, "You know I have a nine bedroom beach house that didn't rent this weekend. Why don't you hold your workshop there? Please be my guests."

I remember walking on the beach early that Saturday morning of the seminar weekend saying to myself, "I can do this!" We had nine people in attendance for my first out-of-state workshop and everyone who had traveled from out of town stayed in the house together.

Overview

Within the pages of *Part II - The Principles & Proofs*, you will discover the importance of understanding the basic laws of creation from a scientific perspective. You will learn that conscious knowledge of this information will allow you to become a conscious creator. This will dispel doubt and move you beyond your wildest expectations.

You will find *Genie* is significantly different from other manifestation books in its attention to understanding the rhythm and flow of cycles, the evolution of scientific knowledge and how this translates to the use of numerical relationships.

Finding the symmetry in the natural order of the Universe will lead to a new awareness of manifestation unlike anything you have ever experienced. Like a cosmic dance, once you learn the steps you will love to go dancing every night of the week. And what's more, you will find you can create your own steps and dances using this same rhythm and flow to your advantage.

When you see there is an order and intention behind what happens in your life you will feel safer living on Planet Earth. What initially appears to be chaotic in your life is really an expression of a mathematical formula that you have set in motion with your intention.

Please take the time to absorb the mathematical and scientific information found in Part II. You may be surprised at the simple explanations. *Be a Genie* workshop participants' comments indicate they believe they would have done much better at math in school if they had learned geometry the way it is presented here. Learning the scientific concepts behind nature will allow your logical, left-brained side to understand the "why" and to make better use of the intuitive, right side of your brain.

The Practices provided you with realistic applications so you would put these ideas into action and start living the life of your dreams. *The Principles & Proofs* will help keep your logical thinking from holding you back. The "yes but," mentality is addressed at the outset. The *Genie System* provides you with formulas for capitalizing on the rhythm and flow of creation. It is possible to create *against* the flow, although the manifestation may be a little slower. But why would you?

Once you know and understand the formula of how to manifest in the direction of the flow of creation, why would you want to work against the current? As any good sailor knows, just turn your sail, adjust your rudder, and use the wind to take you in the direction you want to go. Some directions will not be as swift as others, but forward movement is achievable no matter the wind's direction.

The *Genie System* assists you to follow the flow of conscious creation so that you will turn your inner sail to harness the flow of the energy of the Universe *regardless* of your direction.

Perspective

Belief systems are paramount in this work. In every case the *Genie System* is about gaining perspective, a new perspective that is available to everyone. Changing your perspective can be tricky, but within these pages you will find the tools to make it effortless.

Beliefs allow you to operate in the world. For example, experience may have told you that a house fire is destructive. Yet a fire, properly contained inside a fireplace, provides you with constructive warmth. Your belief that fire can be harmful or helpful is based on your perspective.

You can learn to take a "Fire Walk" where you walk on hot coals without damaging your feet.[47] A fire walk is where you learn to walk on hot coals, without feeling any pain or injuring yourself in any way. The purpose of a fire walk is to learn that it is possible to defy the laws of the Universe. This demonstrates belief systems can be changed.

Logic versus intuition

What are your beliefs? Some of your beliefs are based on religion, others on tradition, still others on actual scientific fact, which is rooted in logic.

Logical reasoning rules in the West. Logic is a good thing, but logical reasoning is not the only way to experience the reality we live in. It allows us to predict the future based on events of the past, but it does not show us how to create a future that is *different* from the past.

Logical reasoning rules in the West. Logic is one way to predict the future, but logical reasoning is not the only way to know what to expect. It allows us to predict the future based on events of the past, but it does not show us how to create a future that is *different* from the past.

---

[47] One such course offered for individuals can be found through the University of Wisconsin, Madison. UW- Madison offers this fire walk class in their outreach program.

Logic is NOT the only way to codify our experience. If you desire to create a different reality than what you are experiencing now, you may wish to try something new.

You probably have had plenty of events happen to you that defied logic, so even though you are taught to think logically, you experience exceptions regularly. Once you begin to view these exceptions as normal, you will find you can easily move between reason and intuitive experience and treat them as equally valid.

Many well-known discoveries and inventions have come through the intuitive state. Elias Howe, who built the first sewing machine, saw his special eye-in-the-point-of-the-needle in a dream. Einstein's theory of relativity was based on a meditation of his recurring dream of what it might be like to ride on a light beam. Dr. Michael Barnsley, who invented the technology used in mini-satellite dishes, discovered his formula to create fractal compression technology in a dream. Who knows how many other discoveries or inventions have come from an intuitive or an altered state of consciousness?

Creating a balance between logic and intuition will enable you to understand the symmetry that is found in the creative force of the Universe. This creative force imbues itself into a crystalline form that has order, symmetry and balance. Once you understand this you can use the *Genie* material to *consciously* create. You will be using both sides of the brain, logic and intuition.

When your logic and intuition begin to work together you will enter a whole new way of being often labeled "whole brain thinking." There are many organizations that are devoted to this whole brain development,[48] and many ways to enhance whole brain activity.

Connecting both sides of the brain will enable you to access and assimilate information that you don't know why you know. It is widely known that the intuitive side of the brain is collecting non-logical data all the time. Your intuitive side doesn't always have the means to turn the information

---

[48] One such organization is the Monroe Institute with its Hemi-Sync® CDs.

it is collecting into meaningful data. Once the logical side allows you to interpret this data, the free flow begins.

This is why whole brain activity is so powerful. In addition, the exercises and intellectual data have been identified to enable you to build more synapses between the left and right hemispheres of your brain. This allows easy access to increase the functionality of both hemispheres.

The *Genie* Practices

In the beginning of this book you learned the five steps that give you the basic formula for manifestation. You discovered the *Genie*'s special meaning of the matrix and lighthouse and how to apply it to your creations. You discovered how groups influence you and how to maintain your own level of influence.

The *Genie System* has taught you about choice and how to become a great director for your movie-of-the-mind. It has shown you how and what to expect, pitfalls to prepare for and what to do when things apparently don't work out. These surprises come in many forms and may be resistance, a fork in the road or may be your Divinity Test!

Finally, we remind you to use the *Genie System*'s unique and powerful method of dealing with fear, no matter what it is. When you discern and integrate these practices in your manifestation work, you will be able to manifest very quickly and become the master over your fear.

Chapter 9, *Tools*, has a list of tools to assist you that have been provided along the way and a few extra tools used uniquely in this work.

Those who have attended my classes or have read the early release of this book have responded enthusiastically with the results of their manifestations. My files are filled with thank you letters from individuals who are achieving their heart's desire and more.

This is another point that I want to underscore. When you use the *Genie System*, opportunities seem to come out of thin air! As in the example at the beginning of this chapter, neither my host nor I had really attempted to solve the small space problem at the physical level. Once the workshop filled, the solution presented itself in the form of an unsolicited offer of the nine bedroom beach house, for free. Not concerning yourself with "How will this work?" is essential to the *Genie System*. This is not to say you abandon the planning stages of any project you are involved in. This instruction is specific to your manifestation work.

The *Genie* Principles & Proofs

Part of the magic of the *Genie* material is its reliance on scientifically proven laws of the Universe, which helps to explain *why* these principles work. Many of the principles found in *Genie* relate directly to scientific concepts such as sacred geometry, quantum mechanics and chaos theory.

Sacred geometry introduces the importance of Phi, the mathematical relationship that is the basis for all of life throughout the Universe. I call Phi "Source Code." By the end of Chapter 14 you may have a big "aha moment" when you learn of the Phoenix Sequence and its implications. That is one of the rewards. The larger reward comes later when you apply this information to your life to make magic.

Quantum mechanics indicates that all possibilities exist. The chaos understanding of the reality recognizes that *feedback* is the source of the Universe's complexity. Throughout the *Genie System*, considerable attention is given to addressing the concept of feedback and controlling it.

In chaos theory, you will learn that feedback *is mathematically occupied* by the Golden Mean[49] and at its core, the foundation of this chaos, Phi. Phi is a mathematical relationship that is found in both organic and inorganic expressions of matter throughout the Universe.

The average person uses less than ten percent of the brain. Using the *Genie System* you will begin to access and use far more of your brain, far more easily than you ever thought possible.

The *Genie System* will show you how and why the basis for all of life is found in Phi. Once you put these principles to work for yourself, you will

---

[49] Reading, Nigel, "Dynamical Symmetries: Mathematical Synthesis between Chaos Theory (Complexity), Fractal Geometry and the Golden Mean," *Architectural Design,* 64: 11/12, 1994, pp. xii-xv.

find you are able to manifest quite easily. *Genie* manifestation is **conscious creation**.

It is as simple as adding one and one to get two. This is the first time a manifestation formula has been expressed in this way. Once you grasp and internalize it, you will be able to apply these principles like a mathematical formula. Then, instead of challenging your logic, it easily supports it.

Chapter 12

The Two Kinds of Creation

Early on in my explorations of the *Genie System*, I decided to use it to win a contest. The objective was to name a new meeting room (function room) for the Princess Hotel Chain. This public meeting room was being constructed at the Southampton Princess in Bermuda. The new construction was a state-of-the-art facility specifically designed for the many medical meetings that were held there.

The contest was open to members of the Association community. My position as CEO of a national professional association made me eligible. A free trip to the hotel was the grand prize. I utilized the techniques in this book. My visual was of me on the beach in front of a beautiful ocean scene. I used a picture I cut out of a magazine with a woman in a beach chair looking out at the ocean. I imagined the hotel behind me was wonderful, and their function room was named the name I had given it. Meditating on it daily at first, the perfect name soon popped into my head, which I then submitted for the contest.

When the winner was announced I was so surprised. It wasn't me! I couldn't believe it. I *knew* my name was the winner. There must be some mistake! I decided not to be upset and forgot about it.

About a year later I was invited on a familiarization tour to Acapulco. The travel agent I was working with told me I had to cover the $100 in taxes, but otherwise the entire trip was free. We would be staying at a first class hotel. I knew this company well enough to know their offer was legitimate and decided to go on the trip.

Upon arriving at the hotel some months later, I was pleasantly surprised. It was the Acapulco Princess. When I entered my room there was a beautiful brochure on the bed showing their brand new meeting room. "Wow," I thought, "this is just like the function room they built last year in Bermuda. They must have used the same architectural blueprint."

I wondered what they had named it. You guessed it. It was the name I had submitted, the one that "didn't win" the naming contest for the Southampton Princess! Here I was, soon to be sitting on the beach, in the hotel that had a meeting room with the name I had submitted for the identical room in Bermuda. And I was a guest of the hotel management! I had received my prize.

Coincidence? Hardly. I had my proof. Here was another manifestation confirming the efficacy of the *Genie System*. There's more hidden in this story. I held no anger or judgment at the "mistake" of not using my name for the contest conference room. I simply let it go.

The two kinds of creation—linear & nonlinear

From my study of sacred geometry I have concluded that there are two types of creation in our world, linear and nonlinear. Everything in this reality is based on a variation of these two methods of creating.

When we see linearly, we are seeing two-dimensionally, or 2-D. Linear creation explains the past and predicts the future. When we see nonlinearly, we perceive our reality three-dimensionally. Because we experience life in three dimensions, or 3-D, we think that everything we see is three-dimensional.

The reality most of us experience is actually the 3-D layered on top of the 2-D, although we are not aware of it. What we see, track and compare is two-dimensional, and from the past. What we see, conjecture and dream about is contained in a world of all possibilities, making the future three-dimensional. Since we experience both as being "in the present," we are seeing 3-D on top of 2-D.

Part II of *Be a Genie* explores this concept of two types of creation from various angles. As you look at certain aspects in life you may discern a linear, 2-D way of perceiving. Other aspects you may see in a nonlinear 3-D way. This nonlinear way may be 3-D, or it may be on a higher dimension than 3-D.

For example, a painter might mix blue and green to get turquoise. If you had no experience with blue or green, only turquoise, how would you know the origin of turquoise? Similarly, the second and third dimensions co-exist, so interwoven into your reality that you cannot see them as separate and distinct dimensions.

An example of linear perception is looking at your past and tracing a line in your history that draws a direct connection between your high school, college experience, your first job, next job, first vacation, etc. You are able to draw this line through time in a linear way; i.e., you attended one high school, not all of them, you attended one college not all that accepted you, etc. If however you were to look at your future through the lens of time you would be looking in all directions at multiple outcomes, if not infinite possibilities.

Creation through the millennia

Many of the world's creation myths lead us to the concept that God created order from nothingness. The ancient Egyptians believed that God created from the void by identifying a boundary around God. This central space led to the creation of the first sphere.

Similarly, from a scientific vantage point, nothing in a void can move, as it has nothing to relate its movement to. Movement always needs a point of reference. If God is everywhere, there is no place God is not. For creation to occur limits must be formed. The first limit is represented as the first sphere. In a void, nothing exists until it has a *relationship*. The first sphere creates self-awareness (Figure 12-1).

So, imagine a limit, or boundary, from a central point extending the same distance in all directions (Figure 12-1). This distance from the central point creates the radius of a personal sphere.

This sphere will be represented in a two-dimensional model as a circle. The sphere now has two awarenesses. The first is everything contained inside the sphere, the second, that which is not in the sphere. Initially both are the same since the sphere was created in the nothingness. However, once something new happens inside the sphere, the two are different. In addition, with all the focus on the inside of the sphere – the outside is forgotten and becomes the unknown. To further expand its consciousness, the sphere reproduces itself. It goes to the limits of its awareness—it's edge—and creates another sphere.

168

Personal Sphere creating the first self-awareness.

Figure 12-1

When the circle goes to its border and reproduces itself, the result is Figure 12-2, two overlapping spheres. They are illustrated as circles. Can you see that the center point of each circle is found on the edge of the other?

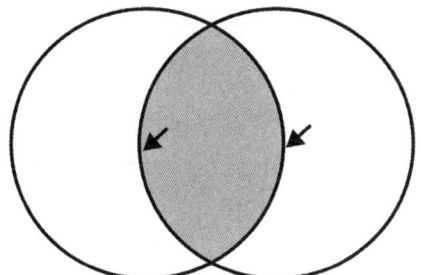

The center point (arrows) of each circle is found on the edge of the other.

Figure 12-2

Vesica Piscis

Once the second circle is drawn, a third entity, the almond-shaped Vesica Piscis (grey shaded area) emerges from the intersection of the two circles. Please keep in mind you are looking at a three-dimensional representation on a two-dimensional medium.

As you examine this magical shape, put your attention on the center shape. Often called the gateway, or Mandorla in art, this almond shape is the basis for all sacred geometry. Although the Vesica is known as the basis for Euclidean Geometry, it can be shown through the evolution of the

169

replication of the circles around this central point to also produce the five Platonic solids.[50]

The Vesica is far more than that. As you look at the diagram above, you can see that there are two identical shapes on either side of a third shape. This central shape, known as a Vesica Piscis (not Pisces like the plural "shape of the fishes") but ONE, distinctly-shaped center. It represents the eternal NOW, your present. Both past and future can be represented on either side, to the left is the past, and to the right is the future.

In the next chapter, look carefully at the photo of the Sacred Mother, the giver of life. Once again you will see that artists from the past chose the Vesica as part of their symbolism to represent the divine mother, source of creation.

The use of the Vesica is found in art, architecture, religion and the occult. This alone would be enough for humanity of today to wonder why it is so sacred. Yet, as a creation template, it represented the womb or vulva. It is the seed source of all form and the form of all seeds! Hidden within the Vesica is the secret to creation. The ancients believed that the Vesica represented **light,** or manifestation itself. Much can be found about the Vesica in Sacred Geometry books. Please know this book is not to train you on the Vesica, or other sacred geometry. My effort here is to educate you with information that is NOT found anywhere else.[51]

I can tell you that I use it in my own work, and have explored this awareness of the Vesica deeply. Consider purchasing sacred geometry designs or artwork, gazing at the mystical beauty and keeping it in a visible place to inspire and uplift you. It will also open your mind to greater knowledge than you can imagine at this time.

---

[50] There are only five Platonic solids: the cube, tetrahedron, octahedron, icosahedron and dodecahedron. Each of the faces of a Platonic solid is identical, producing the same angle and edge length, with the points of the shape inscribing a sphere.
[51] FlowerofLifeBlog.com, *Mary Magdalene Mysteries*. This blog post discusses the Vesica Piscis and its relationship to creation and Mary Magdalene.
http://www.floweroflifeblog.com.

Platonic solids

The five Platonic solids are the core of all crystalline structure, atomic lattices, the periodic table and the very basis of the reality. Amazingly, it is the relationship between each of the Platonic solids that shows us the emergence of the spiral. The Platonic solids in relationship to one another create spirals. Another way to express this is to look at the DNA spiral and notice that you could place the platonic solids along the steps of the DNA ladder.

The Flower of Life emerges

Creation continues to replicate the same circle again and again. Moving from the central point to the edge of the circle, it repeats the process a total of six times to create a circle made up of six circles around a seventh. Interestingly, many of the world's creation myths describe six days of creation, with the seventh being a day of rest.

However something happens as the spheres fall in around a central point. Up until now, all creation has done is repeat itself, always in relationship to itself, creating a sphere of spheres. When this creation process reaches 19 spheres, a new form called the Flower of Life pattern arises.

Flower of Life pattern

As the creation process continues to evolve from its original sphere, a shape or symbol known throughout the world as the Flower of Life pattern emerges with the nineteenth sphere.

Figure 12-3

The creation of the Flower of Life pattern is essentially a cloning process, because the sphere continues to replicate exactly. Cloning is a form of linear progression. One sphere adds to the next based on the equation $y = x + 1$, with "x" being the existing number of circles and "y" being the new number after the cloning. When graphed, this equation forms a straight line. Notice all the almond-shaped Vesica Piscis existing in the Flower of Life design.

Summary

The two kinds of creation are linear and nonlinear. Linear creation, like cloning, is two-dimensional. It relies on the presence of known factors from the past to enable predictable results.

Nonlinear creation is three-dimensional. Plans, dreams and other future events are 3-D because they exist in a world of all possibilities; they cannot be predicted using a linear model.

Myths around the word view creation symbolically as a sphere of consciousness expanding itself by cloning. When two identical spheres overlap sharing the same radius they create a Vesica Piscis. By the nineteenth iteration of the cloning process, a Flower of Life image is formed.

Chapter 13

Sacred Geometry

In October of 2001 (the month after 9/11), I found myself in the unusual circumstance of having an airline ticket for a scheduled workshop that suddenly didn't have enough participants. I had been planning to travel to Tucson, AZ, to give a workshop with a number of employees from the famous Miraval Spa and Resort.

I usually purchase my airline tickets two to three weeks in advance to get the best possible fare. Rarely do I get a "green light" in meditation to purchase a ticket without the final registration numbers supporting it. On the rare occasions when a workshop is held in spite of low attendance, hindsight inevitably shows a compelling reason for being there.

In this case, before the 9/11 disaster in New York City in 2001, I had a good-sized class confirmed. After 9/11, all the individuals who had signed up had had their hours cut at work, due to customer cancellations. One by one, participants withdrew, with the only remaining attendees being the husband and wife who were sponsoring me. I again checked in with my "Higher Self" and was told to go to Tucson anyway.

I could have saved the airfare and used it for a different trip, since I travel so frequently. In a conversation with my good friend, John O'Neil, I remember expressing my surprise at being directed to go anyway. He also felt something calling me to Tucson. He said, "Maureen, I get the feeling that you will be meeting someone." I agreed. I needed to go.

My airline connections took me through Chicago's O'Hare Airport, where I was to make my connecting flight with a few hours of layover. As was my usual pattern, I checked for the gate number several times while walking through the terminals. I sat down at the gate, knowing that there was a departing flight ahead of mine.

After I had been there for some time, engrossed in a project, I felt an inner urge to go to the ticket counter and check the flight. The ticket agent excitedly said, "You missed your flight. Let's see when the next one is… Oh no, they are boarding the only other flight to Tucson **right now**, and you aren't even in the right terminal." He urged me to go there as quickly as possible and promised to call over to the gate to let them know I was coming. I barely made it and received the very last seat on the flight.

In fact, I was so late boarding that the purser had closed the doors before I had my seat belt fastened. Since I couldn't use my cell phone onboard the plane, I sent a mental message to my host that I would be a few hours late and hoped she would understand why I wasn't arriving on the originally scheduled flight.

When I arrived in Tucson, I received a voice mail that said, "Maureen, I trust everything is OK; just let me know when you get in." My hostess had connected with the thought about the missed plane, and had decided to go about the rest of her day and wait for my call.

Sacred geometry's practical applications

While I waited for her to find me near to the front entrance, two gentlemen sat down and began to talk excitedly to each other. Each time I looked at them, their voices lowered, realizing they might be disturbing me.

The third time this happened, I asked my Higher Self,[52] "What's going on?" I was told to speak to them, asking them why they were in Tucson. They said that they had just attended a seminar on day trading in the stock market. They asked me why I was there, and I told them I was leading a workshop on meditation. Their interest instantly dropped. Then I found myself saying, "My workshop is based on sacred geometry." I thought they would fall off their seats. Their trading seminar was also based on sacred geometry. Can you imagine our mutual excitement?

I was thrilled to discover that there are individuals who time their buying and selling of stocks in the stock market based on sacred geometry models. These men apply their science rigorously and make a good income.

---

[52] Accessing your Higher Self can be learned in a workshop or by downloadable coursework through my website. http://www.MaureenStGermain.com

At that moment, I knew why I was in Tucson and why I had missed my earlier flight. Of course I asked to see their workbook, and it became the beginning of a lasting friendship between us, and later with their instructor as well. I have studied their material with their teacher and I see how it works.

In my case, my love of numbers and their properties and expression made me an ideal candidate for finding the symmetry and order in apparently chaotic events.

As I began to uncover these numerical principles, the Universe easily provided more proof that I was on the right track in the form of synchronicity. Synchronicity is coincidence with a deeper meaning because it enables you to see that seemingly unrelated events may be connected.[53]

What is sacred geometry?

Sacred geometry is the study of the relatedness of all things through numerical relationships. When we examine geometry and suddenly see that angles and shapes are replicated throughout nature and the Universe, we have turned geometry into sacred geometry. The place where the Universe reveals its synchronicities to you in number and formula is the place of sacred geometry.

Sacred geometry holds the key to creation in matter. The *Genie System* utilizes this knowledge in a unique way. Manifestation is easy once you understand the mathematical principles of creation and couple them with a mastery of the *Genie* tools.

Part of the reason some people have problems with geometry is that it is taught as theory, without any practical application to real life. It is my intention that you go beyond your present understanding, deep into the symbolism of numbers, the hidden codes of life. Remember, we began

---

[53] Fashioned by Swiss psychiatrist Carl Jung, the term, synchronicity, was used to describe the phenomenon of seemingly unrelated events occurring in unexpected relation to each other where coincidences are not connected by cause and effect but by *simultaneity and meaning.*

using numbers to *represent* something tangible, and it is only our modern society that often requires us to use numbers abstractly.

The early mathematicians and sacred geometry

In America today we have a common "shorthand" phrase in our everyday vernacular. It's 24/7. The phrase actually emerged from the medical field where doctors and nurses referred to their 24-hour shifts as 24/7. 24/7 means that a business or person is available twenty-four hours a day, seven days a week. Its larger meaning has grown to include the idea of "always open." The purpose of bringing up this shorthand is to provide you with a ready metaphor to help you see that numeric shorthand is both understandable and useful.

Our mathematical symbols come from the Pythagorean Brotherhood, the ancient Greek sages,[54] who had their own form of shorthand in their "canon of numbers." This canon was a collection of simple formulas that could also be expressed as ratios and were known as "constants."

Pi or π

A different Greek letter symbolized each formula. These formulas were constant. Just like the Periodic Table of Elements is a set of constant properties of matter, this canon of numbers implied standard mathematical ratios. The Greek symbols were used extensively in their everyday formulas. One familiar constant is Pi, or the Greek shorthand symbol, π.

The reason it is a constant is because its value never changes. Pi became a very useful constant by allowing for the computation of a circle's circumference based upon the easily measured straight line of its radius. Remember your grade school math and the relationship between a circle's radius and its circumference was known as π? When "C" equals the circumference of the circle, and "r" equals its radius, then

$$C = 2\pi r$$

---

[54] The Greeks actually got their mathematics from the Egyptians!

No matter what the size of the circle, the radius and circumference are *always* related to each other in terms of the constant, Pi. Pi represents the **relationship** between a circumference and its radius. Remember this concept, **relationship**, as it will come up over and over again.

The Pythagoreans didn't have the decimal system to allow them to calculate an equation to a certain number of decimal points like we do. These early mathematicians wrote Pi as 22/7. Notice that a fraction is a ratio, a relationship, between two mathematical values. As a result, a ratio that didn't divide evenly (always has a remainder) was always represented as a fraction. Nowadays we describe Pi in the decimal system as 3.14…

Why do we need the ellipsis after the number?

The three decimal points (…) after the number stand for the missing data. It means that the number goes on forever. How does it go on forever? The seven continues to divide into 22 always looking for an exact result, never finding one, and never reaching a precise resolution and always has a remainder. The implication is that these mathematical relationships are never *resolved*. In spite of this non-resolution, the approximation works for practical purposes.

The Greeks were so intrigued by the concept of a ratio such as π—because it could never be resolved fully—that they termed it an "irrational number." Whole numbers, and fractions that could be expressed in a finite way, were "rational." All the rest were "irrational."

Today, a rational number is defined as any real number, which can be written as a ratio of two numbers—a simple fraction—with either a terminating or repeating decimal. For example, 1/4 is considered a rational number because it can be written as .25, which is a **terminating** decimal. 1/3 is considered rational because, even though the threes don't terminate (.3333…), you always know what the next number is because it repeats, thus it is a **repeating** decimal. In the early geometer's mind, knowing that the next digit is the same as the previous one makes it rational.

Phi or Φ

Geometry has two great treasures; one is the theorem of Pythagoras [the formula for finding the hypotenuse of a right triangle]; the other is the division of a line into mean and extreme.

The latter is the ratio that is known as Phi (Φ) or the Golden Mean.

The above words, spoken by Johannes Kepler, the father of the planetary laws of motion, show how mathematicians and scientists have revered these ancient concepts. Kepler had good reason to hold these opinions, as they truly are the basis for modern sacred geometry.

Phi, like Pi, is a member of the Greek canon of numbers and represents an even more valued relationship. Mathematically, Phi never resolves so it is an irrational number, 1.618... Like Pi, it requires a fraction to produce two numbers that are in *relationship,* i.e., like parents, to it. Both ratios (Pi and Phi) require a *relationship* for their very existence. More simply, these irrational numbers are the **result** of a division between two numbers that never gives an exact result, even in decimal form.

Applying sacred geometry

We are so accustomed to interpreting these constants as a number that we have effectively separated a number from the objects it is counting. Numbers are a convention of the mind. They are a way for us to interpret the reality, to allow the mind to encompass vast concepts, but they are only symbols. We use numbers to objectify and quantify our world. As symbols, they can be replaced.

Look into the past

Why were numbers invented? Mostly for commerce. Did you ever hear of someone buying 3.14 cow? Or 1.618 goat? Of course not! Rational numbers are used to express tangible things. Irrational numbers are used to express *relationships.* Understand that irrational numbers, such as Pi and Phi, are part of the family of irrational numbers known as constants, and that their purpose is distinctly different from the original use of numbers.

Knowing this, you can begin to comprehend how special these new relationships, constants, really are.

Magical properties of Phi

What makes Phi so special anyway? There are thousands of books written to answer this question. Two facts that I find most intriguing are: The Golden Mean, by its very nature, is the only division of one (1/1.618) that produces itself whether you are expanding or contracting; the second most important element of Phi is that this relationship can be found throughout nature in both organic and inorganic form. This is a fact we will come back to over and over.

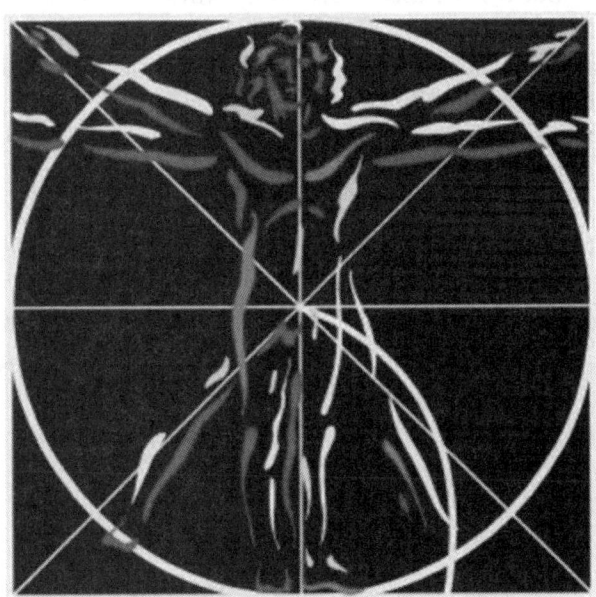

Vitruvian Man by Leonardo da Vinci
Figure 13-1

In early times, Phi was found in the relationship between the different lengths of the bones in the human body. Leonardo da Vinci's Vitruvian Man (*Man in the squared circle*) is one such representation (Figure 13-1). For example, the length of the forearm compared to the length of the upper arm is in Phi.

The name "Golden Mean" or "Golden Rectangle" is used to represent anything that is constructed with Phi as its basis. For example, the front elevation of the Parthenon in Athens is built on a Golden Rectangle. The United Nations building in New York also incorporates Phi in its structure. The Great Pyramid in Giza, Egypt, contains numerous Phi relationships. Many trades require study of the Golden Mean; architects, artists, dentists, to name a few.

How to create Phi

The Golden Mean rectangle is based on Phi. To build one, first draw a square. Find the center point in the baseline of that square (A) and draw a line to one of the corners (B). Let that line become a radius of a circle (arrows). Allow that arc of the circle to continue to the base of the square (C). Draw a perpendicular line at this point and extend lines at the top and bottom of the square (D) to create a rectangle from the square. Voilà. You have a Golden Mean rectangle (Figure 13-2).

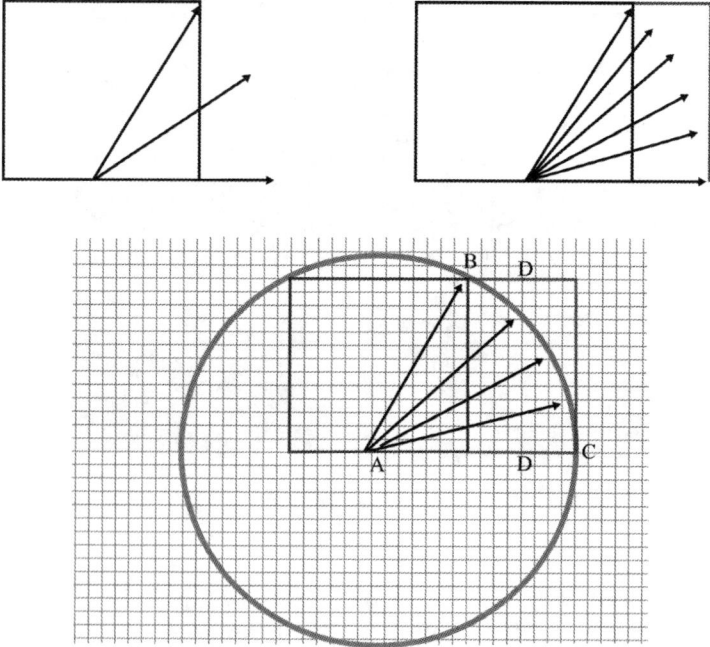

The Golden Mean rectangle construction
The ratio between the long side and the short side
is in Phi ratio.

Figure 13-2

Phi is the relationship between the length of a Golden Mean rectangle and its width. Not surprisingly, when a Golden Mean rectangle is divided by Phi, it creates another smaller Golden Mean rectangle. That is, the two rectangles are scaled versions of each other. There's that most important element, again. Every division of Phi reproduces Phi. This is why the ancients were so fascinated by Phi.

Modern computing has continued to reveal to us more and more places the Phi ratio can be detected. It is found in the DNA spiral, the curve of an ocean wave and the spiral arm of a galaxy.

**Golden Mean is found in the spiral of the ocean wave.
(Photo – Philippe deFouchier)**

Figure 13-3

Summary

Sacred geometry is the study of the divine shapes and relationships in both organic and inorganic forms. Sacred geometry is the understanding of numbers, their relationships and their expressions.

Pi and Phi are two of the most important numerical relationships in all of creation. In decimal form, Pi is 3.14... and Phi is 1.618...They are called irrational numbers because when the division implied in the ratio is calculated, neither Pi nor Phi can resolve into a number with a terminating or repeating decimal. These constants are irrational numbers and are expressed as the symbols π and φ, respectively.

The *Genie System* shows you how to use these symbols conceptually, and in applications to other aspects of your life that aren't numeric in expression. In so doing, you will be learning to apply sacred geometry to your manifestation work.

The constant Phi is expressed in both living organisms and in such things as the curl of an ocean wave and the spiral arms of galaxies. Revered by both ancient and modern mathematicians, the deeper meanings behind Phi and its expression throughout nature are still being discovered today.

In the *Genie System* you will apply two important properties to irrational numbers: (1) they always require the presence of "parent" numbers; and (2) they never resolve, always leaving a remainder.

You will use Phi conceptually in your manifestation work as you explore the Fibonacci and Phoenix Sequences in the next chapter.

Chapter 14

The Phoenix Factor: Introducing Fibonacci and the Phoenix Sequence

Debbie Ashworth finished her Master's of Education degree but skipped her graduation ceremony to attend a *Genie* workshop. She had just gone through a difficult divorce and felt that the manifestation workshop would be just the ticket.

Within one year's time of attending, she changed jobs, started a career as a motivational speaker, married the man of her dreams, traveled through Europe for a month-long honeymoon and much, much more. This is just a partial list from her thank you letter to me just one year after attending. She understood the *Genie System* and put it to use for herself.

History of numbers and the pyramids

The twelfth-century mathematician Leonardo of Pisa, nicknamed "Fibonacci," is credited with being the source of one of the most well-known sequence of numbers, which is named for him. Historically speaking, the Fibonacci sequence itself predates his disclosure in the year 1202, by more than a millennium, having arisen around 200 BC in the work of the Hindu Pingala.[55]

While on a visit to Egypt to study the pyramids, Fibonacci was most impressed with the Arabic knowledge of the pyramids. He learned how they valued Phi and its alter ego the Golden Proportion, or Golden Mean. Fibonacci became enchanted with the Arabic awareness of Phi and included this knowledge in his widely circulated book, *Liber Abaci.*[56]

---

[55] Fibonacci is also credited with converting the West from using the cumbersome Roman numerals to the more functional Arabic numerals.
[56] In the original sequence, Fibonacci describes the number of pairs of rabbits *n* months after a single pair begins breeding, assuming the offspring begin breeding when they are two months old. This was first described by Leonardo of Pisa (Fibonacci) in his book, *Liber Abaci.*

The Arabs showed him how Phi ratios permeate the structure of the Great Pyramid of Giza, and all living things. One example of the Phi ratio in the Great Pyramid is illustrated below (Figure 14-1). Fibonacci's studies with these Arabs led him to look for Phi relationships everywhere.

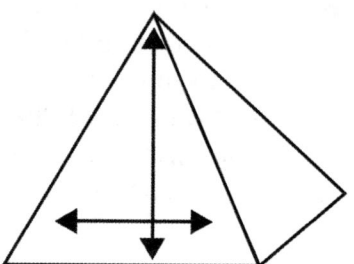

The relationship between the height of any side of the Great Pyramid of Giza is in Phi ratio to the length of one side of its base.

Figure 14-1

When a Golden Rectangle is formed, the relationship between the long side and short side is Phi. This Golden Rectangle can be subdivided into Phi, creating another Golden Mean Rectangle. If you connect the arcs drawn from each division of the long line a spiral emerges. This spiral continues infinitely both inward and outward (Figure 14-2).

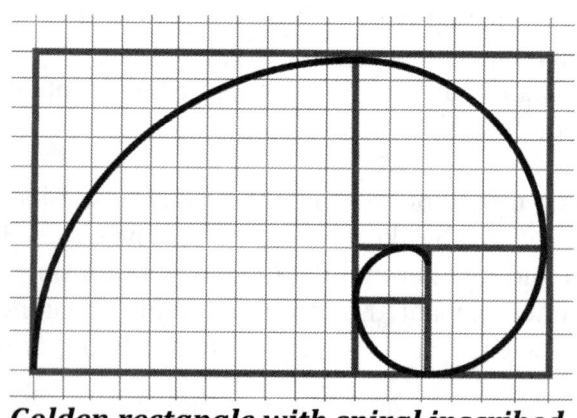

Golden rectangle with spiral inscribed

Figure 14-2

184

Why is Fibonacci so important?

Fibonacci is the name of a sequence, based on the notion that the plant kingdom grows in a fashion that replicated this specific sequence. This sequence is 1, 1, 2, 3, 5, 8, 13, 21, 34, 55... Although this sequence carried his name for centuries, its earliest known documentation came from the Hindu Pingalia. Fibonacci is credited with this because he wrote about it in his book, *Liber Abaci*. He later won the equivalent of the Nobel Prize for this work, which eventually convinced the west of the benefit of converting from the use of Roman numerals to Arabic numerals. He was actually describing how rabbits reproduce!

Notice that it starts with one, then the one duplicates itself, and then adds it to itself to create two. This sequence continues by always adding any number in the sequence to its preceding number to arrive at the *next* number in the sequence.

> ### *1, 1, 2, 3, 5, 8, 13, 21, 34, 55, 89, 144...*

Fibonacci sequence
Figure 14-3

One can easily see that the next number in the sequence above is 233. No matter where you are on the sequence you can find the next number in the sequence simply by adding any two adjacent numbers. These last two numbers in the Fibonacci sequence become the "mommy" and the "daddy" to the next number in the sequence.

Many plants grow in this orderly sequence. Consider the rose, a modern day example. First it grows a stem of one leaf, then two, then three, then five and then the rose bush throws a bud.

Turn to any rose-growing manual and it will tell you **not** to cut below the five-leaf stem. If you do, the rose will have to grow another five-leaf stem before it throws a bud. This rose growth pattern has been written about and passed around from gardener to gardener for centuries.

Rarely will you be told that the leaves are producing the Fibonacci sequence and that after five leaves the rose throws a bud and starts over. Yet it is the rose's unique expression of the Fibonacci sequence.

Echinacea (Cone Flower) has 13 petals.

Many of the numbers found on the Fibonacci sequence are found in the petals of flowers such as daisies, corn marigolds, dahlias, morning glories, and cone flowers (Echinacea). This discovery led to the understanding of what the ancients had known but revealed only enigmatically.

Hibiscus (above left) and Mandevila (above right) both have five petals.

Again, let us look at the sequence:

> ### 1, 1, 2, 3, 5, 8, 13, 21, 34, 55, 89, 144, etc.
>
> *As you examine this sequence, note that morning glories have five petals, daisies have 21 or 34 petals, dahlias have 34 or 55 petals, and so on.*

Figure 14-4

Looking at Phi through Fibonacci

Here we see that nature has found a new way to create besides repeating itself as in cloning. In this form, nature looks to its previous creation and instead of simply repeating itself, as in cloning; it *adds itself* to its previous value to create the next number (i.e. 2 + 3 = 5). The second number "1" in the sequence looks like a clone of the first one but the first "1" is actually being added to zero to get the second "1". Every number after "1" is unique (Figure 14-4).

This sequence is unique for a number of reasons. It is linear because it follows a simple addition of terms in a sequence and produces a straight line when it is graphed. In creating the sequence, it uses the previous two numbers to create the third one, thus it takes nothing outside of itself. This principle of adding the results of one computation to create the next is called recursive.

The Fibonacci sequence is also nonlinear, as **each adjacent pair** in the sequence produces the irrational number Phi, one of the most important numbers in the canon of the early geometers.

How Phi and nature are connected

It provides a new understanding of the numerical pattern in creation because it embodies both rational and irrational numbers. As you move up the sequence you continue to create whole numbers, however dividing any two adjacent numbers produces an approximation of Phi, 1.618.... The Fibonacci sequence embodies *Phi*.

The ratio between any adjacent pair always approximates Phi. The higher up in the sequence, the closer the ratio comes to the actual value of Phi. No calculation can ever exactly express Phi, because it is an irrational number, the result of a *relationship*, an abstract concept always with a remainder.

We can use the relationship between two adjacent numbers of the Fibonacci sequence to express Phi (Figure 14-5).

Picking up the sequence mid-stream we find:

$$34/21 = 1.61904$$
$$55/34 = 1.61764$$
$$89/55 = 1.61818$$
$$144/89 = 1.61797$$

which shows us the relationship to Phi,1.618...

If you were to chart the above results of division on a graph, they would snake around an invisible line moving closer and closer to the actual line (represented by Phi), yet never landing on it.

Figure 14-5

By examining the *relationship* between the adjacent numbers, a new form, a spiral, is created.

Nature provides us with the ability to see a spiral being created. As you look at spirals coming from whirling vortexes like water going down the drain, or leaves growing around the central stem (phytoaxis), you can perceive the height, width, and depth of the spiral.

The spiral drawn on a flat paper needs perspective to create a clear visual image of its true form. What makes a spiral unique is its property of change. It has an element of evolution in it.

In addition, the Fibonacci sequence approximates the Phi spiral. If you represent the sequence on graph paper by successive right-angled lines, with lengths proportional to the number in the sequence, the Fibonacci spiral coincides with the Phi spiral between the eighth and ninth iteration

(Figure 14-6). Why between the two? Because all irrational numbers are not numbers, but *relationships*. Relationship implies the contrast between two things, producing the outcome that always has a remainder. This shows how the Fibonacci sequence is also a nonlinear means of creation.

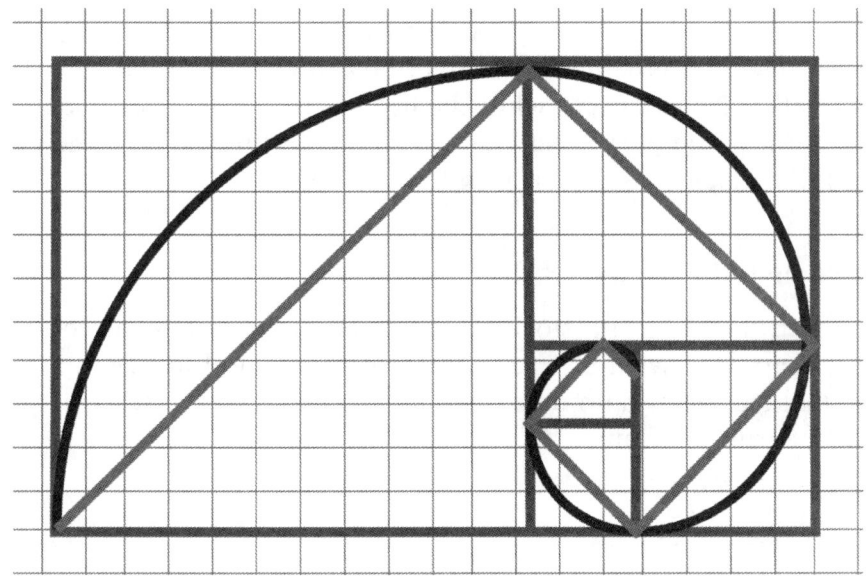

Phi spiral & Fibonacci spiral superimposed.

Figure 14-6

Finding Phi in nature

In the previous chapter you were introduced to Phi and how it occurs throughout nature. Phi is found in both organic and inorganic matter all over our world.

The sequence laid down by Fibonacci is seen in the growth of the chambers of the nautilus shell. If you look closely at a cross section, the heart of it is a single tiny chamber, which you can define as "1". The next tiny chamber—also "1"—is at right angles to the first. After the next turn, the chamber is twice as large, "2", while the next turn's chamber is "3", then "5" and so on.

When you look at a pinecone's counter-rotating spirals of seed caps, you will find the same pattern of growth.[57] This relationship also can be found in comparing bones of the body, celestial orbits[58] and the relationship between leaves of a growing plant.[59]

Even our DNA reveals Phi/Fibonacci in its structure. Being submicroscopic, DNA is measured in angstroms.[60] The diameter of the DNA circle is 21 angstroms while the height, measuring from one full turn of the spiral to the next exactly above, is 34 angstroms. Thus the ratio of the spiral's dimensions, 34/21, is in Phi.

Where else do we use Phi?

Remember the successful stock traders I met in the Tucson airport? Their teacher, Larry Pesavento,[61] uses a photo of Michelle Pfeiffer as a sample of the Golden Mean ratio on a "perfect" face. Why? Because the perfect human face always features the ratio of Phi!

---

[57] The Fibonacci numbers are sometimes called pinecone numbers, according to Theoni Pappas. This is because the opposing spirals that appear on the pinecone are always two successive Fibonacci sequence numbers. (Pappas, Theoni, "The Fibonacci Sequence & Nature," *The Joy of Mathematics*, San Carlos, CA: Wide World Publ./Tetra, 1989, pp. 224.)

[58] In charting the relative speed of Earth, Jupiter and Saturn, Phi is revealed to a stunning 99.99% accuracy. (Marineau, John, *A Little Book of Coincidence,* Walker & Co; April 2002, p. 46.)

[59] Scientists continue to discover that not only do the leaves in a sequence produce Phi, but that the Golden Ratio can be found through the measure of the fraction of a turn between successive leaves on the stalk of a plant. The Fibonacci sequence ratios are: 1/2 for elm and linden, 1/3 for beech and hazel, 2/5 for oak and apple, 3/8 for poplar and rose, 5/13 for willow and almond, etc. (Coxeter, H. S. M., "The Golden Section and Phyllotaxis." Ch. 11 in *Introduction to Geometry*, 2nd ed. New York: Wiley, 1969, Ball, W. W. R. and Coxeter, H. S. M., *Mathematical Recreations and Essays*, 13th ed. New York: Dover, 1987, pp. 56-57.)

[60] An angstrom is one ten-billionth of a meter (or 0.0001 micron).

[61] Larry Pesavento is author of over 20 books on Sacred Geometry and the divine ratios used for day trading on the stock market and trainer to thousands who have successfully adopted his methods.

Studies on human psychology also confirm our preference for this natural order and symmetry and the relationship we find in Phi.[62] It is not the only sacred geometry number, but it is the focus and central key in the *Genie System.*

Magical properties of Phi

Phi has another unique property. If you divide the ninth (55) and tenth (89) iteration on the Fibonacci sequence the result is 1.618... If you reverse the ratio and divide 55 by 89 the result is 0.618... This irrational number is known as phi (lower case p).

Phi and phi are reciprocals of each other. Phi is the only irrational number or relationship that expresses this property.[63] This is how the Phi spiral is created. Phi spirals expand infinitely inward with phi and infinitely outward with Phi.

Mean and extreme division of a line

The ratio of AC to AB is Phi;
the ratio of BC to AB is also Phi.

Figure 14-7

---

[62] In 1876 Gustav Fechner, a pioneer in the field of experimental psychology, conducted a famous experiment wherein he asked a statistically significant number of people to rank their preferences for a series of rectangles. Among the 10 shapes shown to the subjects, ranging from a square to a double square, the overwhelming preference was for the Golden Rectangle, which is based on Phi.
[63] By convention, Phi (Φ, capital 'P') is 1.618...; while phi (φ, lower case 'p') is 0.618..., the reciprocal of Phi.

Imagine a line divided up into Phi ratio (Figure 14-7). If the smaller part is defined as 1 then the larger part is Phi, or 1.618... The larger portion is in Phi ratio to the entire length. So the whole provides the same relationship as the smaller part to the larger part.

Assume B x ϕ = A
then
A:B as (A+B) is to A

Figure 14-8

This is a cardinal feature of *Phi*. There is only one proportional division of "One" possible using two terms, with the third being "One" itself.[64] No other division can produce Phi in this cyclical manner. Therefore, Phi contains all the information about itself in every part of itself. That is, it is holographic.[65]

Power of three

Recently, the History Channel's popular show, **Ancient Aliens**, featured a segment on the incredibly consistent evidence of the number three or "sets of three" throughout art, literature, architecture and more.

Included here is a photo from an original chapel asp at the Cloisters Museum.[66] It shows a very common image of the Vesica, with the three wise men on one side and the Annunciation depicted on the other. The fact that Mary is in the middle is one very important element, and another is that she is pictured inside that magical shape, the Vesica.

---

[64] Euclid, *Elements,* Book Five, Theorem Three (Alexandria, 3rd century BC): "A straight line is said to have been cut in extreme and mean ratio when, as the whole line is to the greater segment, so is the greater to the less."

[65] Holography is a photographic technique that captures three-dimensional objects on film and then projects them into space to form 3-D images that look like the real thing. The holographic film captures the object from different angles and distributes the information into all of the parts of the film. Thus, if you cut such a film into halves or fourths, it will still be able to project the same image.

[66] The Cloisters, a branch of the Metropolitan Museum of Art, was built in the 1930s resembling architectural elements of several European medieval abbeys. It contains original structures, facades of both inner and outer recovered medieval chapels and many artifacts.

To examine the Phoenix Sequence more closely, let us start with **any** two random numbers. Add them together, and then add in a cyclic fashion producing a result, each time adding the result to the previous result. Repeat this process ten times. The final adjacent pair produces Phi. This is stunning! Try it for yourself!

Not only can you produce Phi from the Fibonacci sequence, you can produce ˙˙ from every Phoenix Sequence by dividing any two adjacent num˙˙s in this sequence after the ninth and tenth iteration. The ˙˙oenix Sequence always creates this magical number Phi, no ˙˙ ˙˙er what two numbers you start with.

By using this bluepr˙˙ ˙˙you will produce Phi every time you have completed 10 repetit˙˙ ˙˙nd created a ratio from the last two numbers. Sometimes a ˙˙ ˙˙approximation to Phi will show up before the tenth iteratio˙ ˙˙pends upon how close the original two numbers are to each ˙

Feedback and the Phoenix ˙

Every Phoenix Sequence **relies u˙** ˙˙ **results of the equation to calculate the next number.** It relies ˙˙back from the prior result to get the next result. This is again the us˙ ˙˙irrati˙˙. Current number, previous number and new result are the key to the ˙˙x Sequence.

Another way to predict the next number ˙ All Phoenix Sequence is to multiply the current number by 1.618… and ˙ sig˙ to the nearest integer.

Chapter 8 discussed feedback in much greater ˙ Her˙ ˙ow you can see the dramatic importance of producing Phi through ˙˙ ˙eans, because the feedback comes from within the system. Usin˙ **En**˙ing data from a formula for the next computation is called recursive ˙ wh˙ity of feedback that produces Phi from a Phoenix Sequence.

Using the Phoenix Sequence, you can now apply it to a manifestation matrix.

Yesterday	***Today***	***Tomorrow***
Past	***Present***	***Future***

Past x Phi = Present.
Present x Phi = Future.

***Using the principle of feedback from the model of the
Phoenix Sequence, you create the next number
based on the previous two.***
***Using the feedback from the past and present
to create the future is central to the Genie work.***
***Finally, you will be introduced to the formula that
shows you how to use the two outside numbers,
(Past and Future) to insure an outcome which
becomes your new Present.***

Figure 14-10

When you apply this method to your manifestation matrix, the *past* multiplied by Phi creates the *present*, and the *past* in relationship to the *future* produces Phi, thus guaranteeing the *present* to be in perfect harmony with your heart's desire. Thus, looking at the *past* allows you to view in two dimensions, and looking at the *future* allows you to see into three dimensions. Looking back into the *past* you can see a straight line from one event to another. Looking into the *future* you have multiple possibilities, multiple directions. The *present* is the result of Phi acting on the *past*. By the same token, the *present* multiplied by Phi creates the *future*. Using this knowledge, called the Phoenix Sequence, you will unlock the secret of manifestation.

The Phoenix Sequence is a term I coined to establish the meaning and value of the recursive additions producing Phi. Even though you may have read of it elsewhere (it's been "borrowed"), it started with me, defining it in the original version of *this* book, *You are the Genie in the Bottle,* back in 1994 when it was first released in manuscript form.

Summary

Fibonacci is inaccurately credited with discovering the mathematical sequence that bears his name. This sequence begins 1, 1, 2, 3, 5, 8, 13, 21, 34, 55, etc. and goes on infinitely. It is calculated by adding the last two numbers together to find the next one.

Fibonacci also studied the sacred geometry of the Great Pyramid in Egypt, noting all the Phi relationships in its structure. He was known for many things including convincing Europeans to shift from the use of Roman Numerals and adopt "Arabic" numbers and their numeric system based on ten.

The Fibonacci sequence is important because it is found in both organic and inorganic matter. It determines the growth pattern of all life, from the molecular level of the DNA to the cosmic level of galaxies, and is directly related to spirals. The fact that this relationship permeates all of creation gives pause for thought, and holds the key for manifestation!

The Fibonacci sequence approximates growth based on Phi and can be used to calculate an estimate of the Golden Mean, Phi.

Phi (1.618...) and phi (0.618...) are reciprocals. Spirals are another expression of Phi, swirling infinitely inward with phi and infinitely outward with Phi. Phi, by its very nature, replicates itself in relationship to itself.

The Fibonacci sequence is not the only way to produce Phi mathematically. It is a specific one belonging to the class of sequences that follow this same formula. I call this class of sequences the "Phoenix Sequence". The Fibonacci sequence is a Phoenix Sequence.

An estimate of Phi can be derived from every Phoenix Sequence carried out to the ninth and tenth iteration by creating a ratio of the last two numbers. The Fibonacci sequence is one of the most easily identified versions of the Phoenix Sequence that nature uses to create.

Phoenix Sequences rely on feedback to perpetuate themselves. They rely on the previous results to create the next result. This quality is named recursive and represents feedback.

197

Another way to predict the next number in any Phoenix Sequence is to multiply the current number by Phi and round to the nearest integer.

When you apply this method to your manifestation matrix, the past multiplied by Phi creates the *present*. The present multiplied by Phi creates the *future*. When you allow yourself to hold onto two versions of the reality, past and future, you will ride the Phi rainbow into your heart's desire. This is the secret of manifestation.

Chapter 15

Understanding Creation in a New Light

In 1994, one of my sons and his friend wrote a computer program for me to produce the fractal known as the Julia Set (See Chapter 16). They were eighth graders and they knew of my high interest in fractals, their relationship to nature and their scientific link to chaos theory. I wasn't the only one on this trail.

A fractal is a mathematical representation of chaos. A fractal is a geometric structure that provides detail at every scale of magnification and thus cannot be represented by classical geometry. Aptly named Fractal Geometry, it is a product of a nonlinear, or chaotic, system.

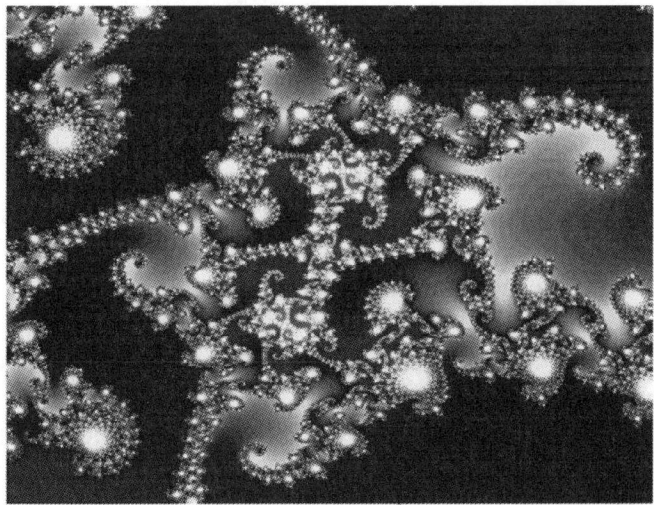

Fractal

Above is a photo I generated of a fractal system based on the Julia Set. Anyone can make these with wonderful fractal software that is available either for sale or as shareware.

Figure 15-1

Chaos theory

In the early years of chaos theory, 1960's mathematicians and scientists alike didn't even know what to call their newly emerging science. Up until then, most of science relied upon neat rules that followed specific immutable laws that produced predictable results, cause and effect. Anything that couldn't be explained or predicted was ignored for the most part.

Newtonian mechanics tells us *distance equals velocity multiplied by time* (Figure 15-2). We all have used this fairly regularly whenever we drive a long distance. When we know we are going 60 miles per hour, we easily calculate the distance we have driven by dividing the time.

$$D = V \times T$$

Figure 15-2

This formula, derived from Newton's Second Law of Motion, shows us that if we increase our speed we will proportionately increase the distance traveled in a set amount of time. Alternately, if we wish to reach our destination sooner, we increase the speed. This is called a linear equation. Small changes in linear systems cause small predictable results. Big changes cause big results. If you put more sugar in a recipe it will be sweeter. If you cook a cake longer it will be dry or burned. These linear equations produce incremental, predictable results.

Mathematics and science rely on proven theorems and formulas. Newtonian physics easily describes the motions of two celestial bodies in space, but it fails utterly when attempting to describe the simultaneous motions of three bodies. This is the famous "three body problem," also known as "deterministic chaos."

Chaotic systems

An emerging science aptly named *chaos theory* that could offer explanations for fluid dynamics and other dynamic systems appeared on the scene that didn't follow the standard rules of "cause and effect," such as the *three body problem*.

This science was derived from the study of weather forecasting—a clearly chaotic system. During World War II, the military assigned mathematician Edward Lorenz to develop a model to forecast weather. The military needed weather forecasters for tactical planning of air, sea, and ground movements. At that time, experts believed that if they could only find the right model, they could use a series of equations to describe a dynamic system such as the weather. By collecting data on all the variables, e.g., wind velocity, temperature, humidity, sunspots, and air pressure, they would be able to make long-range weather predictions. The models developed had limited success.

After the war, Lorenz began to work as a researcher, writing software programs to emulate the weather. It was believed that making use of the massive calculating power of the early Cray computers would enable these researchers to write programs to emulate the weather. This was based on their belief and understanding of linear systems. They felt they could input all the causes into a weather system and get a prediction of the resulting weather. These systems, with their multiple causes and effects, turned out to be different from linear systems.

How a new science is born

One day, Lorenz decided to re-run a program he had developed for long-range weather forecasting. As the story goes, returning from a coffee break, Lorenz discovered the printer paper had run out. He restarted the printing and picked up the equation midstream. This was a number with approximately nine decimal places, so he picked up the calculations midstream dropping off the last few places.

The end result was significantly different from his previous result *even though he had used the exact same set of equations*. The identical program should have produced an identical result. This aberration led Lorenz to question what had just occurred. Finally, Lorenz realized the only changed factor between the two sets of calculations was the use of the rounded off numbers. This led him to the dramatic conclusion that minuscule, or very small changes, in a dynamic system could cause widely divergent results.

When Lorenz presented his finding at a 1972 meeting, he called his talk, "Predictability: Does the Flap of a Butterfly's Wings in Brazil set off a

Tornado in Texas?" And thus this phenomenon was dubbed the "Butterfly Effect." The following graph illustrates this concept.

Dynamic system graph

*The two lines are meant to be the same
until an unpredictable turn occurs.*

Figure 15-3

Changing the way we understand the reality

The implications of Lorenz's Butterfly effect were astounding and led to a dramatic change in the way in which experts approached dynamic systems. While Lorenz knew that complicated dynamic systems are determined by their causes, the big surprise was that new causes are constantly folding in on themselves. Once scientists realized this, chaos theory was born and utilized to study all those dynamic systems that could not be explained using the old linear models.

"New" causes appeared to come in a form of feedback that influenced the system in unpredictable ways. This was a dramatic departure from previous science that depended upon knowing all the causes in a system to determine its outcome. This folding in on itself—**feedback**—had never been considered before.

The *Genie System* of manifestation requires understanding the natural world around you and applying these scientific principles to your own understanding of the nature of manifesting and creating. Controlling feedback is crucial. In the *Genie System*, you are learning to control your feedback in ways you have never considered before.

A linear system is illustrated by the following graph of the equation Distance = Velocity X Time.

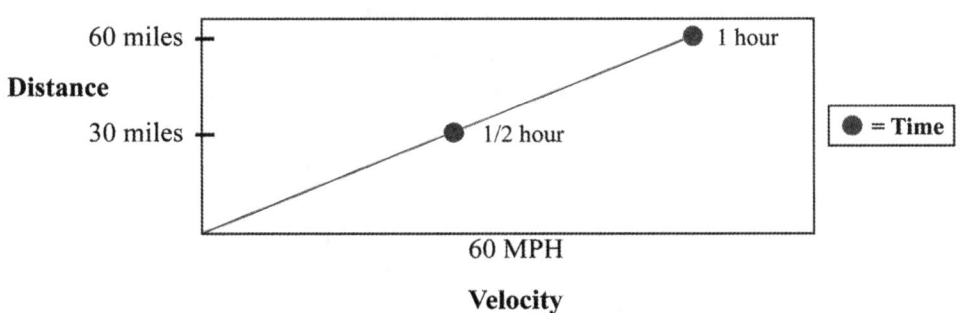

Distance = Velocity X Time

Distance equals Velocity times Time.
With a constant speed of 60 MPH,
in one hour the distance traveled is 60 miles.

Figure 15-4

Linear systems and non-linear systems

All linear equations are logical, incremental and predictable. They are formulas that can be described by linear mathematical equations, which form a straight line when graphed

In contrast, as the name implies, nonlinear systems are defined as systems that change radically through internal feedback. As chaos theory developed, scientists began to understand that the major unpredictable element of any system was its feedback.

Chaos theory shows that in nonlinear systems, the folding and refolding of feedback quickly magnifies small changes so that the initial cause, like a small rolling snowball that starts an avalanche, seems completely out of proportion to its effect.

Nonlinear systems behave this way because they are so webbed with feedback that the slightest twitch anywhere may become amplified into an unexpected convulsion or transformation. Negative feedback keeps a system static, positive feedback causes sudden dramatic change.

Negative feedback is any feedback that keeps a system static. Positive feedback is feedback that causes a system to move, shift or change. The study of chaos led to the realization that under some circumstances nonlinear systems behave in a regular, cyclical way, supported by "negative feedback" which keeps the system orderly. Orderly, that is, until something sets it off, a critical point is passed, and suddenly the system is chaotic. The chaos is supported or created by "positive feedback" which allows the dynamic system to jump out of its predictability.[68]

Think of the game of pick-up sticks you may have played as a child. The game is to take turns with other players to keep picking up one more stick from the pile, without having the pile come crashing down. The negative feedback keeps the pile in place. The positive feedback causes the avalanche of sticks to come crashing down. These two tables illustrate this point:

Linear & dynamic systems

Class	Linear	Nonlinear or Dynamic
Proponents & Examples	Newton's Laws Kepler's Laws	Max Plank, Niels Bohr, Chaos Theory & Quantum Mechanics
Feeling Appearance	Stable Predictable	Alternating Stable and Unstable Unpredictable
When graphed	Straight line	Curved–although it may waver around an imaginary column

Figure 15-5

Two kinds of creation, looking at cause & effect

	Cause	Effect
Linear	Small changes Large Changes	Small Effects Large Effects
Dynamic	Small Changes	Seemingly Random Large Effects Due to Feedback

Figure 15-6

---

[68] Jumping out of predictability is one of the key factors you will use in your *Genie* work.

How does this chaos/feedback impact the *Genie System*?

As discussed in the last chapter, you are becoming more and more aware of the importance of "feedback." As taught in the Phoenix Sequence, feedback in the system is essential. As long as the feedback comes from the original pair and their offspring, the two original numbers are all that is needed to produce the feedback loop resulting in Phi from the 9th and 10th resulting ratio.

Remember that controlling feedback is one of the most important elements of manifesting. Outside influences can occur. It is up to you to recognize if this feedback is a match for your system or not a match. If it's a match, you decide their level of influence. This is controlling feedback. You control your outcome by controlling feedback.

Summary

Chaos theory has enabled science to explain behaviors in the physical Universe that had been largely unexplained and *ignored*. It provided a new understanding of the reality that enabled experts to recognize that miniscule causes in a system could produce large effects, seemingly out of proportion to the original cause. Such feedback would keep a system static until, suddenly, it would burst forth with dramatic shifts caused by the seemingly miniscule feedback.

In Chapter 16, The Quantum Connection, you will begin to crystalize in your mind how the connection to this new science of chaos theory applies to your manifestations. When you choose to control feedback, you control the manifestation. Once you understand how feedback works mathematically, both for you and against you, you will start to pay attention to it.

Remember that feedback is important and we will apply it proactively using the Phoenix Sequence.

Chapter 16

The Quantum Connection

Quantum physics

Quantum physics provides more science to support your creations. It is the area of physics that defines the behavior of subatomic particles, called quanta. The conundrum in quantum physics is that even though quantum mechanics has proven to be highly predictive and accurate, it doesn't seem to represent the reality we experience every day.

In an experiment first conducted in 1801 by Thomas Young, and later explained by Max Planck's graduate thesis almost 100 years later on quantum theory, you will find a sample of the quantum quandary.[69]

The experiment involved beaming light through a slit in a screen. A photographic plate was set up to record the light after it passed through. The resulting image on the plate was a predictable replica of the same shape as the original slit. The DVD, *The Secret*,[70] has a nice graphic explanation of this experiment that plagued science for almost a century.

However, when there were two parallel slits, the light created an entirely different image on the photographic film. It looked more like a waveform interference pattern of curved sections of light and dark, as if the particles had traveled through *both* slits at the same time (Figure 16-1).[71] Yet when detectors were placed at the slits, particles moved through one or the other slit, but not both. These two-slit images indicated light has wavelike properties, also.

---

[69] Planck was awarded the Nobel Prize for his theory, 18 years after announcing it in 1900.

[70] *The Secret* (Extended Edition) starring Rhonda Byrne, Bob Proctor, Rev. Dr. Michael Beckwith, et al. (2006).

[71] Woodborough 2000, named Crop Circle of the Year (2000), photo courtesy Lucy Pringle, Author, aerial photographer, researcher and world-wide lecturer. The UK's most comprehensive crop circle photographic library at website: www.lucypringle.co.uk.

Why, might we ask, was the crop circle from 2000 (Figure 16-1), remarkably similar to this very same geometric shape formed by the two slits? The combination of light and dark lines are the result of the waves coming through both slits and canceling each other out in some places and emphasizing each other in others.

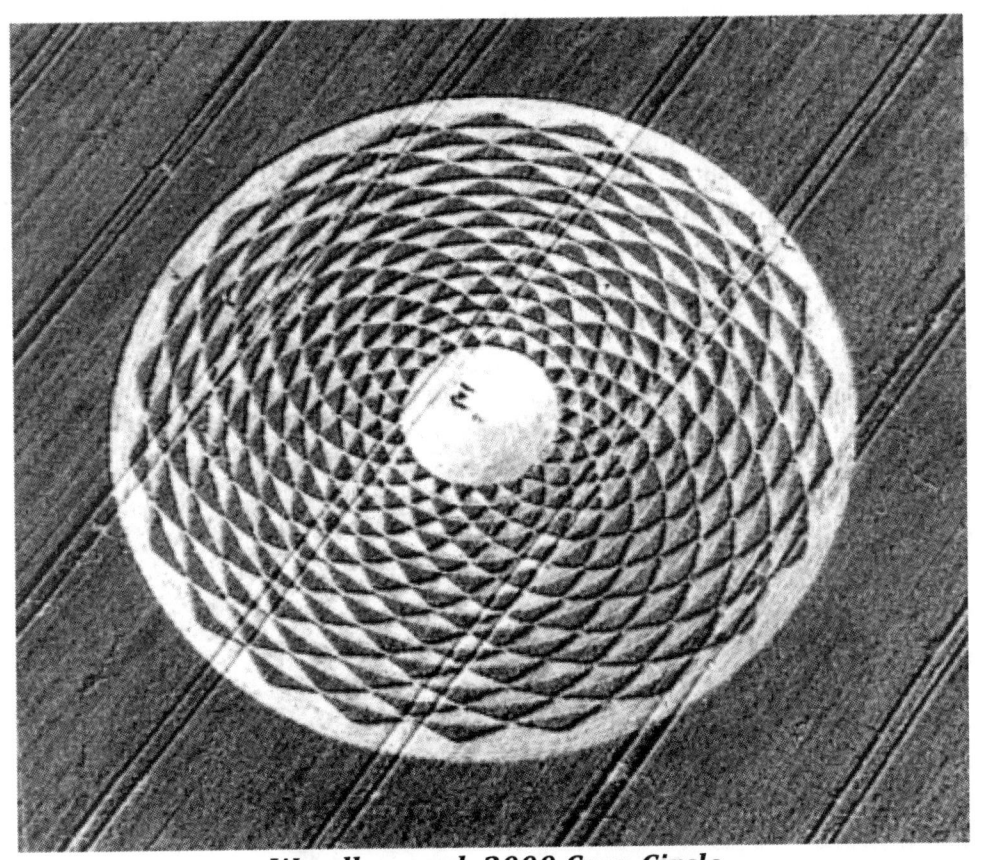

Woodborough 2000 Crop Circle
(Photo © Lucy Pringle)
Figure 16-1

This pattern of crossing light and dark produces this amazing logarithmic pattern on concentric circles, in relationship to the center.

The word quantum, as applied to physics, is implying anything that is smaller than the atom. This means all available data is acquired by electron microscopes and changes our perspective.

All possibilities exist

One of the basic concepts of quantum mechanics is that all possibilities exist and it is the observed reality that is being experienced.[72] The observation can vary by the type of equipment used. One of the permutations is the "collapse model" which states that all other versions of the reality cease to exist as one particular version is observed.

This seems a bit counter-intuitive, because it implies that as one version is *observed* it rules out the possibility of other versions existing at the same time. Physicists like Niels Bohr assert that it is ONLY the act of observation that turns any quanta into a particle, and that the quantum "soup"—the place where all possibilities exist—is made only of waves. He further asserts waves of all kinds have particle counterparts, a concept that is still under scrutiny.

Physicists like David Bohm tell us there is an order that can be found in the Universe and that electrons are not just particles or waves, but highly complex entities capable of responding to consciousness and matter.[73]

Some modern physicists, such as David Deutsch in the UK, have long held that a multi-Universe is the only adequate explanation of the findings of quantum physics. By this he means that **all possibilities** exist, period. As a mystic, my take on this is slightly different. Multiple versions of the reality exist, not infinite, as might be implied by Deutch, but a limited number. I can also tell you that this "number of possible versions of the reality are controlled by you - by your own need to experiment - at all levels of consciousness.

---

[72] The observer, as part of the equation, is both widely regarded and widely disputed by physicists.
[73] David Bohm was a physicist with the University of London. He was a protégé of Einstein's and was one of the world's most respected quantum physicists.

Expectations influence results

According to Deutsch, it is the instruments we use to observe and measure the phenomenon, as well as our *beliefs* about it, that limit the possibilities from multiple to one possibility. At the same time, he also postulates that the very act of observation affects the *visible* Universe.

Marilyn Schlitz, Director of Research at the Institute of Noetic Sciences, has shown that experimenter expectations significantly skew the results of psi tests.[74]

Further study of quantum mechanics has led to experiments that concluded that if a researcher **intended** to measure a particle, and used equipment that measured particles, then particles would appear, and if the intention was to measure a wave, and used equipment that measured waves, then waves would appear.

The observer effect

The effect the observer has on what is observed is critical to understanding manifestation. One thing is certain; the quantum field always accepts what is seeded into it.

Physicists now acknowledge the process of observation has an effect on the final outcome at the subatomic level.[75] Yet most believe this principle does not operate at the level of everyday life. They conclude that the subatomic represents one version of the reality, and the physical world operates by a set rules established by Newton and others that bear no resemblance to the quantum view. They are unable to bridge the two realities.

If you find this mind-boggling, know that many brilliant physicists are still baffled by the apparent incongruity of the explanations of quantum physics. It appears that the more they learn about the reality, the more

---

[74] Schlitz, Marilyn, *Experimenter Effects and Replication in Psi Research*, http://noetic.org/blog/experimenter-effects-and-replication-in-psi-resear/.
[75] Heisenberg, Werner, *Uncertainty Paper*, 1927. Heisenberg's Uncertainty Principle states: "The more precisely the position [of a particle] is determined, the less precisely the momentum is known."

their understanding opposes the basic laws of the Universe as laid out by Kepler and Newton.

Multiple dimensions may be the explanation

The explanation may lie within the concept of dimensions. I believe that as we become more aware of our dimensional existence, we may discover that we co-exist in multiple dimensions. Hence, Newton's Laws of Motion and Einstein's Theory of Relativity could represent a valid reality from the two-dimensional world. If this two-dimensional world co-exists within a three-dimensional world that is explained by the rules of quantum physics, then perhaps the dimensions exist inside of one another in a nested sort of way.

Scientists have attempted to address this enigma by explaining that the very act of observation causes all the possible states of a particle/wave to "collapse" abruptly into a single value, which specifies the position and the wave or particle nature it manifests.

To quote David Deutsch again, "It [quantum mechanics] is probably the most powerful, accurate and predictive scientific theory ever developed. Despite unrivaled empirical success of quantum theory, the very suggestion that it be literally true as a description of nature is still greeted with cynicism, incomprehension and even anger."[76]

Modern physics – what have we overlooked?

Theorists, who limit quantum physics to the subatomic world, would have us believe that their rules apply only to the sub-atomic "stuff" of which we are made up and not to the larger, readily-observed reality.

Could it be that our ability to gain *perspective* from observing our world through a particle physicist's instruments has enabled us to gain a view of the reality unavailable to us through our senses? By achieving a larger view of something very small, we have gained perspective—a clearer view of our world and ourselves.

---

[76] Deutsch, David, *"Comment on 'Many Minds,' Interpretations of Quantum Mechanics by Michael Lockwood,"* British Journal for the Philosophy of Science, 47 222-8 (1996).

Although modern theorists largely ignored the implications of quantum physics, there are estimates that some thirty percent of the United States' gross national product is derived from some sort of technology based on quantum mechanics. This includes such everyday necessities as cell phones, CD players, and portable computers.[77] Where does all this lead? It leads us to the conclusions of David Deutsch, who states, "All possible events, all conceivable variations on our lives, must exist."[78] Wow.

Quantum mechanics applied to *Genie* manifestation

We use this proven scientific principle—that all possibilities exist, and that intention is a significant element in outcome—in our *Genie* work. It is a profound key to manifesting.

Once you grasp the concept that all possibilities exist all the time, then you can begin to understand that you have **choice**. You have the ability to direct your attention to certain outcomes that will take you *to and beyond* your heart's desire. Remember this, as it is essential to our Genie Manifestation.

When you look back from a vantage point in the future, which is beyond your heart's desire event, you will see a chain of events including the desired one. From this vantage point you are observing your desired outcome as a *past event*. In the next chapter, this is simplified into a numerical equation so we can examine it more closely.

Believing is seeing

Researchers have known that there is a blind spot in the visual data collected by the retina in the eye. It has been identified and quantified. The eyes cannot see anything that is in the location of the blind spot and the brain will "fill in" with the surrounding data.

Because this blind spot has been identified, researchers now believe that the brain may be selectively editing what we see in other areas as well. Perhaps, "believing is seeing."

---

[77] Ibid.
[78] *Discover Magazine*, September 2001, pp. 38-39.

However, this fails to explain the following story based on the log of Antonio Pigafetta, a member of Magellan's crew:

When Magellan's fleet passed through what was later named the Strait of Magellan... they anchored off the shores of what they called "Tierra del Fuego." Upon rowing to shore in small dinghies, crewmembers discovered that the Native inhabitants of Tierra del Fuego were amazed at the crew's seemingly sudden appearance onshore. Some of the Natives pointed to the sky in wonder: had Magellan's crew descended from the heavens? No, of course not—they had arrived in the large, masted ships anchored in the harbor. This claim, however, would require some careful and patient explanation on the parts of the crew as well as the village visionaries (seers), because to the majority of the people living onshore, there was nothing at all in the harbor. The people of Tierra del Fuego, having never seen anything like the large ships anchored in plain sight, were unable to see those ships. It was not until their minds were prepared to perceive something previously unknown and un-encountered, that the people onshore were finally able to see the ships in their harbors.

The rules that govern human perception are strange and vague and they beg the question of how - how is it possible that the shamans or visionaries of Tierra del Fuego could see the impossible ships in the harbor but those not accustomed to perceiving alternate dimensions could not?

How, for that matter, can one look at something and not actually see what is visibly there?[79]

Neither on land or sea had the Native peoples seen anything that closely resembled his ships in size. Perhaps their brains ruled out any possibility of them existing.

Science has shown us that it is possible that we are already collecting data with our eyes that our brain is selectively deleting or ignoring. When we

[79] Sparrowdancer, Mary, "Challenging Views and Changing Perceptions", 2001, at http://www.sparrowdancer.com/perception.html.

create an atmosphere of acceptance we can then receive and interpret data that previously passed right through us.

We may be doing the very same thing with quantum mechanics. How would we know?

The *Genie* material requires you to look at the reality from a perspective that includes all possibilities. Think of your first driving lessons. You may remember how you, as an inexperienced driver of a car, would over-steer, resulting in your car wobbling all over the road. Very quickly you learned, or someone told you, to look beyond the car and to focus well out in front of the car in order to steer effectively. Expanding the view of your path enabled you to drive with the road *in perspective.*

The greater perspective we have gained from looking at the quantum world has enabled us to create a larger view of the reality at our level. Another way to illustrate a larger view of the reality is to turn to driver's education. When I was learning to drive an automobile I was over-steering, causing the car to wobble. The instructor showed how we use perspective to make sure we drive where we want to go, and instead of looking directly in front of the car, I was guided to expand my view and look further out. More recently, I went riding on a motorcycle and the driver pointed out that the perspective changes, and you must look even FURTHER out. Remember this concept, as it is important to gain the larger view.

Perspective and fractals

In the late 1960's, French mathematician Benoit Mandelbrot found a way to generate a visual image of the feedback found in chaos using the massive computing capacity of the early mainframe computers. Mandelbrot named his pictures "fractals" and a whole new understanding of chaos began.

By assigning color values to pixels on a screen, the formula system used feedback to create colored patterns within patterns that kept repeating as they grew. Mathematicians weren't prepared for the astounding results they achieved in creating fractals. Fractals have beauty, form and, most importantly, a "self-similarity" not hinted at or expected.

Fractals have enabled science to gain a new perspective by seeing the order and symmetry coming out of chaos. The millions of iterations[80] of a complex formula reveal a view of chaos showing its intrinsic symmetry and order! Thus, feedback is central to the system. Modern mathematics calls this function "recursive" (Figure 16-2).

Start with a Formula (small flat end) the result is the smallest arrow (1). Second arrow's starting point is the flat end (2) that expands and curves upward. Third arrow begins its flat point (3) moving around the smaller one. This form of iteration builds on the successive computations of each addition, like a dog chasing its tail.

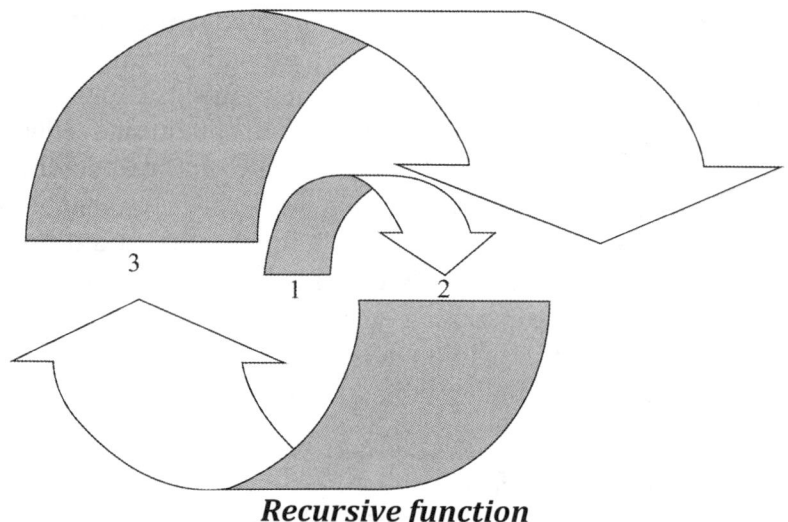

Recursive function

Figure 16-2

Even though a fractal is constantly growing like an irrational number's decimal place that will never resolve, a fractal pattern has order, beauty and symmetry that is easily discerned. The further away the pattern is—or the greater the magnification—the more the order in the "big picture" emerges! By "zooming in" to see the microcosm, or "zooming out" to see the macrocosm, the intrinsic order in our everyday world is made visible.

---

[80] The formula for producing the Mandelbrot set is based on a recursive formula: $f(n+1)=f(n)^2 +c$, where c is a constant.

As you look at the Julia Set, a well-known fractal, you can see the same shapes at all scales from the whole picture to the tiniest detail. How was it possible that an unpredictable dynamic system could continue to show self-similar shapes throughout the computation? (Figures 16-3 and 16-4) Perhaps the answer lies in feedback!

Fractals, and the chaos systems they exemplify, like the Phoenix Sequence, rely on adding the current result to the previous result to get the next one. Feedback from the previous computation is necessary to get the next value. This is true whether you are creating Phi with the Fibonacci or Phoenix Sequence or whether you are creating fractals.

Fractals have shown us the order in chaos based on perspective. What if there is another facet to the complex process called feedback? What if all possibilities exist until one version receives feedback that tips the scales its way?

If the deciding factor in quantum physics is the nonlinear feedback, then feedback plays a central role in the construction of the reality, whether it is the quantum world, the fractal world, or our everyday world. And if all possibilities co-exist, then all things must be connected and therefore a part of a much larger whole.

The Julia Set

Fractals are a way to visually see the "self-similarity" found in nature. (Julia Set is both Figure 16-3 and Figure 16-4, as they are ever changing/evolving pictures.)

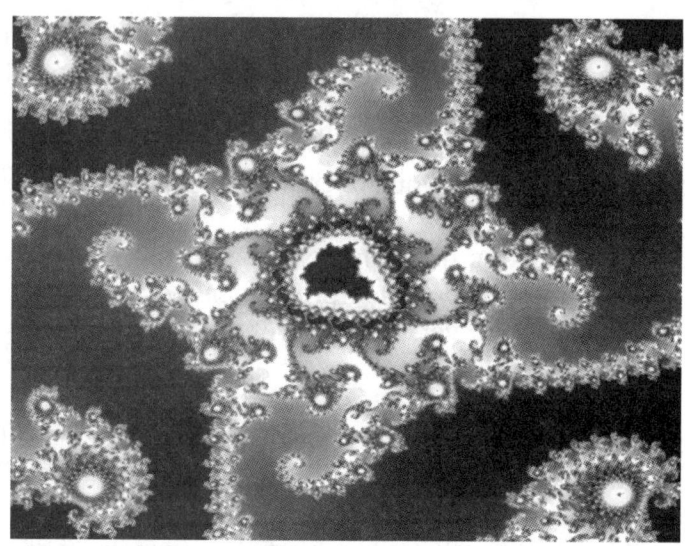

Figure 16-3

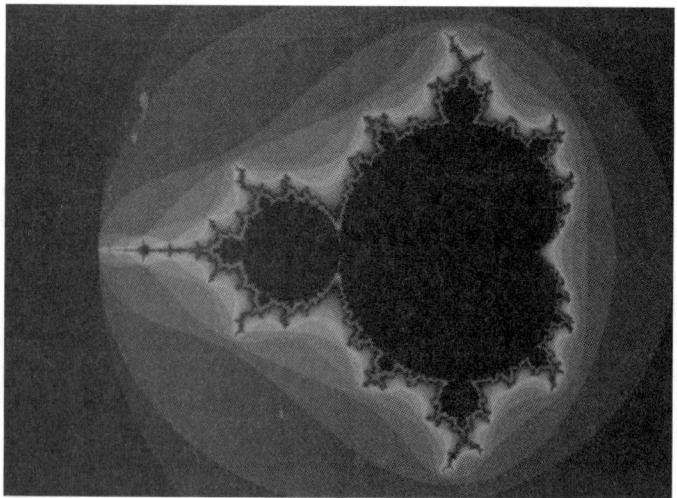

Figure 16-4

Summary

Quantum physics provides the scientific basis to support your creations.

Quantum physics, which is the study of subatomic particles, also accurately describes the reality in a much larger context. It states that all possibilities exist, that intention affects reality and that the observer can influence that which is observed.

Although most scientists have difficulty accepting all of the implications of quantum theory, there are some who insist that if we are made up of particles—which we are—and if quantum theory has proven to be infallible in every conceivable experiment—and it has—then it must be true of the physical world that we observe.

Quantum physics also appears to contradict Newton's Laws of Motion and Einstein's Theory of Relativity. How can that be?

We co-exist in multiple dimensions. Newton's laws and Einstein's theory represent a valid reality in the two-dimensional world. This two-dimensional world co-exists within a three-dimensional world explained by the rules of quantum physics.

We have gained *perspective* from observing our world through a particle physicist's instruments.

Fractals, a pictorial representation of chaos in which patterns repeat in every level, have also shown us a new perspective. Zooming in to see the microcosm, or zooming out to see the macrocosm, makes the intrinsic order in our everyday world visible. Fractals have beauty, form and, most importantly, a "self-similarity."

Nonlinear feedback, in the form of observation, allows the observer to play a central role in the construction of the reality.

Science has demonstrated that you are already collecting data with your eyes that your brain selectively deletes or ignores. When you create an atmosphere of acceptance you can then receive and interpret data that previously passed right through you.

You can interact in the reality in ways that defy traditional science. These new methods are now being supported by a whole new wave of science. Once you integrate this information, manifesting your heart's desire will be a matter of **choice** not chance.

Chapter 17

Order in the Universe

One day, several months after I had taken my car to a body shop to have several minor dents repaired, I noticed that the front end was full of little nicks. I thought, "Gee, I should have gotten the front end touched up at the same time as the back end. I really wish I had a new front end." I didn't do anything about it because I had just left my full time job and didn't want to spend the money. I was about to discover just how powerful at manifesting I had become.

The very next day, while driving in the middle of the afternoon, a deer jumped in front of my car. I was able to slow down, but it still did enough damage that I had to have the hood replaced and some front-end work done. I pulled over to inspect the damage. A woman behind me stopped to see if I was OK. She told me, "I drive to and from work on this road every day and have NEVER seen a deer at this time of day."

I felt OK, and my car was drivable, so we each got back into our cars and headed down the road. Less than 1,000 feet away, on the other side of the hill, was a policeman writing a ticket for some speeder. I pulled in behind him, hoping that he would give me a police report for me to turn in to my insurance company.

My new friend who had been following me pulled over, too. Synchronistically, she was a friend of the officer, reported the whole story to him, and within fifteen minutes I was on my way with the necessary police report. The only thing it cost me was my deductible and 15 minutes of my time.

Learning through the ages

Throughout the first six chapters of *Genie,* Part II, you have followed some of man's progress in attempting to understand the Universe. Some theories have been revolutionizing, some less dramatic, yet all fall within the context of trying to make sense of it all.

Western science and religion have been at odds on and off through the centuries. The Roman Church decreed that Divine Revelation, as interpreted by the Church, was the only source of Truth. However, the Church's "Divine Revelation" was often based on superstition and speculation.

The scientific method

The scientific method emerged from an era when the "authority" was the church. It presented an objective alternative to this religious stranglehold and effectively created a new freedom of thought. The 16th century scholar, Sir Francis Bacon, known as the father of inductive reasoning, codified the scientific method as the unbiased means to prove the validity of a hypothesis.

The scientific method is a very effective tool with which to study the world, and it became the benchmark by which everything else was proven. It was successful in its goal to release the monopoly the church had on all communicated knowledge. Eventually the scientific method made it possible for anyone to investigate and develop theories that peers could review, replicate, and accept as true.

Copernicus, who knew the Earth revolved around the Sun, risked his life to state this fact in a world ruled by Earth-centered Church dogma. It was this very controlled, intellectually stifling environment that produced the demand for change that led to the scientific revolution.

Newton, who benefited from this new freedom of information, described a world that was mechanistic, and which followed basic laws of motion that revolutionized Western thought.

Eventually, flaws were found in Newtonian mechanics. In 1887, Albert Michelson, physicist and professor at Case School of Applied Science in Cleveland, joined forces with Edward Morley to conduct the famous Michelson-Morley experiment to measure the effects of "ether drift" on light.

Newton's laws of motion assumed there was a universal reference frame—ether. They predicted that the speed of light should vary based upon whether the ether drift was in the direction of the light or away from it. Even though the Michelson-Morley experiment found no difference, subsequently, the M-M experiment turned out to be flawed and inaccurate,[81] even though some physics textbooks still don't acknowledge that.[82]

This asks us to lean into the idea that science isn't nearly as tangible as we thought. Another source states, "Mainstream science tells us the Aether does not exist because it is not physical. However, mainstream science talks about 'electrical currents' and 'twisted magnetic field lines' as though they were physical objects...current is not a physical object of itself. Also, magnetic field lines are considered by mainstream science to be mathematical structures, not physical structures."[83]

The return of intuition

Now science and intuition seem to be merging into accord. The pop culture book, "blink",[84] reads as if there were a new wave of scientific information about how to live life based on a new groundswell recognizing the *intuitive*. Malcolm Gladwell says in his forward, "But what would happen if we took our instincts seriously? ...we would end up with a different and better world."

In the introduction of the book, Gladwell tells a tale of a forged museum piece that the Getty Museum in California authenticated, and then realized via "expert's" intuitive reactions that it was a forgery, a ten million dollar forgery.

---

[81] http://lgsims96.hubpages.com/hub/Michelson-Morley-Experiment
[82] Bryson, Bill, *A Short History of Nearly Everything,* Broadway; 2003.
[83] http://www.unexplained-mysteries.com/column.php?id=216792
[84] Gladwell, Malcolm, "blink*" the Power of thinking without thinking,* 2005

"I always considered scientific opinion more objective than aesthetic judgments…Now I realize I was wrong."

- Marion True,
Curator of Antiquities,
J. Paul Getty Museum

The time has come for us to give equal weight to both sides of the brain. Both sides of the brain gather information – but the West's preference for logic over intuition has caused us to stray too far from the middle.

Enter chaos theory

Chaos theory states there is order in chaos. In most of the world's creation myths, including the Book of Genesis, God is described as having moved on the face of the deep (chaos) to bring light (order). Science is now corroborating religion. Amazing!

Much of the "new" information has come from the last century. Yet, at the beginning of the 20th Century, some scientists felt that there was very little left to be discovered.[85]

This hubris was quickly undermined by Max Planck's quantum theory and Einstein's Theory of Relativity, which replaced Newtonian mechanics as the new model of the Universe. What has become clear is that no matter how much we know today, we will know more tomorrow.

The scientific method, which began as an orderly system for understanding our reality from an objective stance, has now become the only legitimate way of knowledge. Rather than balancing with the divine revelation of religion, science ultimately discredited intuitive knowing. Eventually, the scientific method began to invalidate all information that could not be objectively measured. As a result, internal states and data derived from intuition were rejected as "not scientifically verifiable" and

---

[85] Albert Michelson, the first American to win a Nobel Prize, believed that the work of science was nearly at an end, with "only a few turrets and pinnacles to be added, a few roof bosses to be carved," as quoted in *Nature*. (Bryson, Bill, *A Short History of Nearly Everything,* Broadway; 2003.)

222

therefore not studied. The intuitive way, the feminine way of gaining knowledge, was discredited and abandoned. The scientific revolution, which began as an open-minded solution to the religious stranglehold, is now the oppressor of free thought.

Modern scientists actually employ the feminine way; they just don't talk about it very much. The feminine way is the intuitive way, the meaningful dream, the hunch that won't go away. The feminine way is often given a back seat to the logical way.

Many books have been written comparing the feminine way of looking at reality with the masculine way. The scientific method, as it stands today, is not the only way to gain knowledge. It is one way. It is the intellectual, male-oriented way. Now is the time to integrate both the masculine and feminine way. Satisfy the mind, but mind the intuition.

Integration

My intent here is to help you to integrate the masculine and feminine ways to create balance. When you expand to give equal weight to subjective as well as objective data you create with balance. This balanced form of gaining and using knowledge is integral to the *Genie System*.

This approach involves simultaneously applying the principles of feminine creation, by using emotion with visual images, with the masculine principles of reason, science, and math to create a framework that supports your creation.

This method creates harmony within your mind, resolving the learned tendency of logic to prevail. In the past, you may have used visualization to create with your intuitive right side, only to have the logical left side say, "Yes, but…" and undo your creation. When you are using both logic and intuition together, your manifestations will occur with greater speed and ease because you won't be taking one step backward for every two forward steps.

Connection to all of life

When you restore the balance between the masculine and feminine ways of knowing, you will become more connected to all of life. What does it mean to be connected to all of life?

Saints and sages have pondered this question over the ages. In the larger view, if we are all connected, why do we feel so separate? Consider that we may have purposefully separated from God in order to gain knowledge.

Our reality is created in order for us to "experience" something. Life is about experiencing parts of the whole. You and I deliberately separated from what is, essentially, inseparable in order to gain experiences. These experiences are to be valued highly. I honor this, and invite you to do the same.

Surpassing limitations

In the case of mass consciousness, we have collectively agreed on a certain order to our world, such as the laws of science. Time is one of these mass consciousness limitations we have agreed on, but even that law can be circumvented.

There are always vehicles to move you beyond any constraint, depending upon the individuals and the circumstances. You have discovered inside these pages a number of "time barrier" stories that helped you see the elasticity of your reality.

Your ability to manifest is directly related to your ability to influence the "space" around you. You have absolute control over what thoughts you allow in your head. You have the ability to redefine your reality. The more strongly you give yourself "permission" to go beyond your limiting beliefs, the more accurately your creation will reflect your desires.

Summary

The scientific method emerged in Western civilization during the 16th century as an alternative to the authority of the church. Sir Francis Bacon codified the scientific method as the unbiased means to prove the validity of a hypothesis.

The masculine, mechanistic world described by Newton, made way for the relativistic world of Einstein. Now, even Einstein's theories are being challenged, and rightly so.

The feminine way is the intuitive way, the meaningful dream, the hunch that won't go away. It is re-emerging as a valid approach to knowing. In many cases, even the masculine solution to a mechanical problem comes through the dream time.

It is time to integrate the masculine and feminine ways. When you expand the scientific method to give equal weight to subjective as well as objective data you create with balance. This balanced manner of gaining and using knowledge is integral to the *Genie System*.

When you restore the balance between the masculine and feminine ways of knowing, you will become more connected to all of life.

Our mass consciousness subscribes to a certain order to our world, such as the laws of science. Time is one of the limitations we have agreed on, but even that law is elastic.

Conclusion – Update 2013

In closing, what I have learned in the years since I first wrote this book is that we are still on the frontier of manifestation. I believe that many of the tools we have sought are within our reach.

In Part I of the book, *The Practices*, I have given you all the tools, methods and practices that were developed after I discovered the Phoenix Sequence. My customers and I have used these tools successfully for years. You can too.

In Part II of the book, *The Principles & Proofs*, I provided the details and scientific principles that support the *Genie* manifestation system.

Why even bother with the Phoenix Sequence? Once you integrate this knowledge, your logical side will step back, allowing the underlying symmetry of the Universe to be understood mathematically. This knowledge, based in the logical side of the brain, will enable you to relax, get out of your own way and allow you to go about the business of creating what you really desire.

When this book was originally written, Part II of the book came first. Initially I thought everyone would love to read about sacred geometry, quantum physics and more **before** learning the practices. I realized later that many just wanted to jump into this sea of manifestation right away to experience what they could do. Most who read the early release of this book agreed that reading *The Practices* first would be a good idea. This is why I reversed the order of the book.

Now that you have read Part II and understand the importance of the scientific principles behind the *Genie System*, I suggest you go back and read Part I again because now *The Practices* will have a practical, logical basis. You may wish to think of Part I as **your** instruction manual and Part II as **God's** owner manual.

Thank you for allowing me to present the *Genie System* to you. I wish you a Day of Heaven on Earth every day for you and everyone you meet.